Enjoying this notebook?

Please leave a review because we would love to know your thoughts, feedback, and opinions to create better paper products for you! Share how you creatively use your notebooks, journals, and stationery products.

Thank you so much for your support. **You are awesome!**

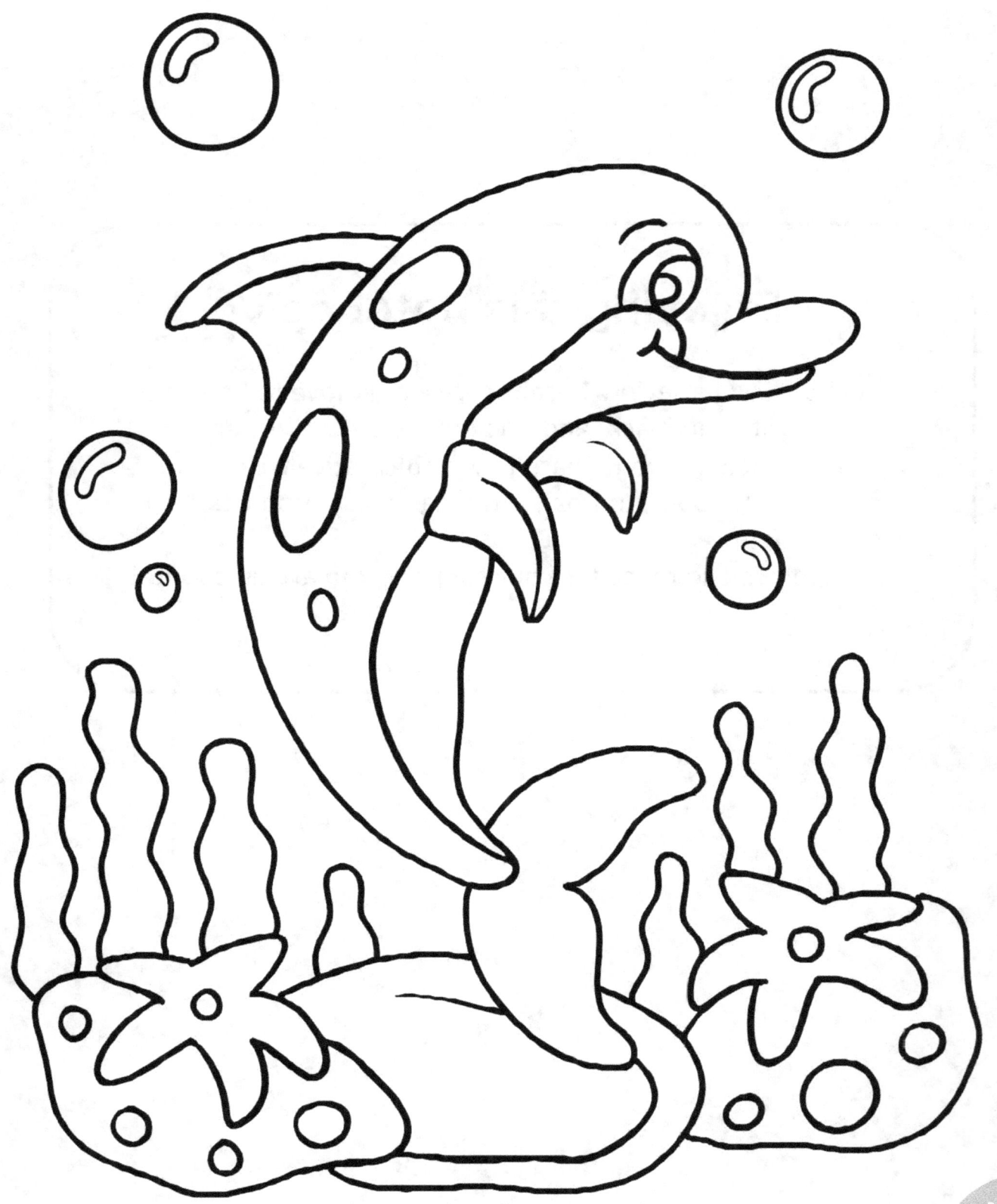

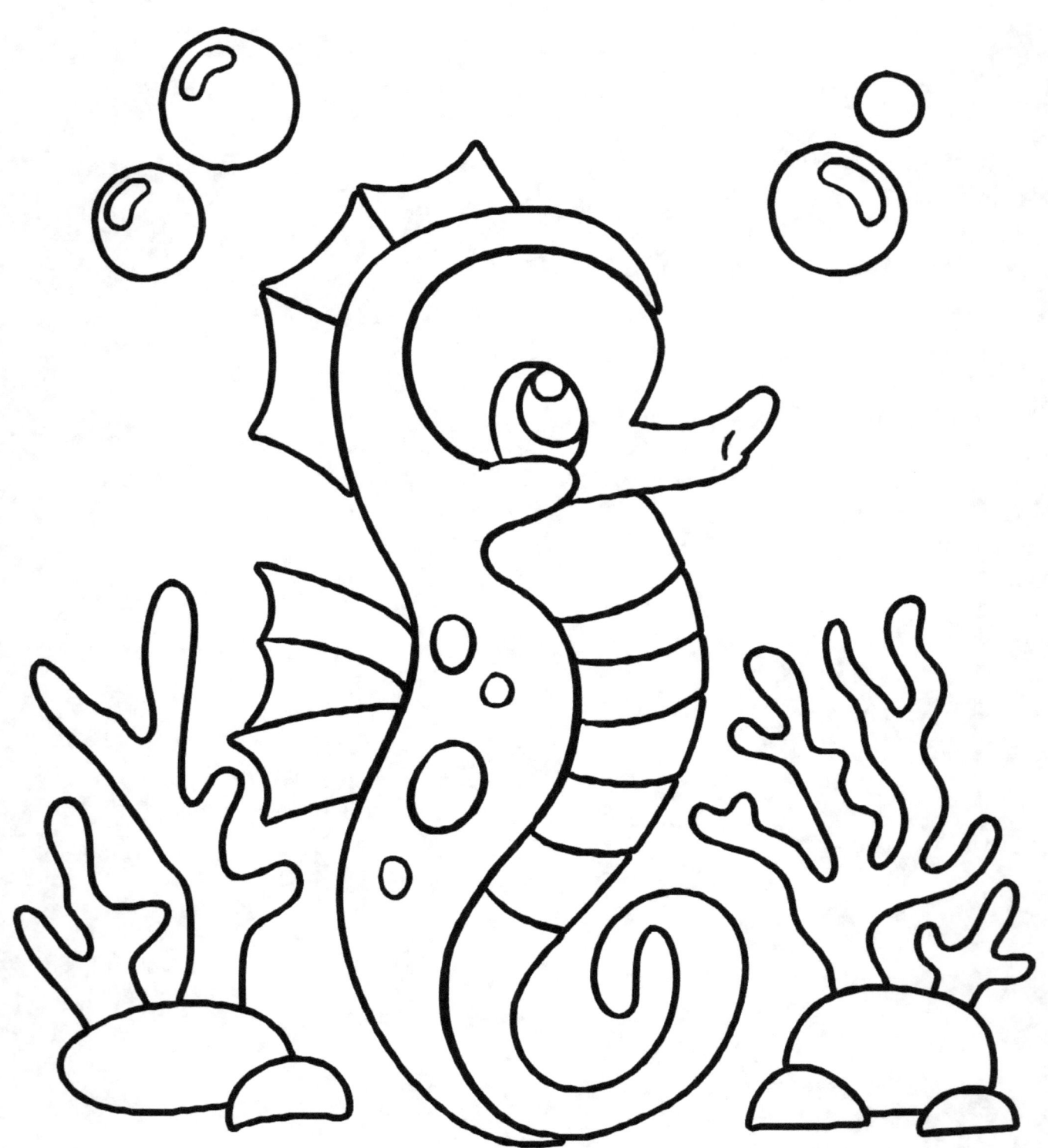

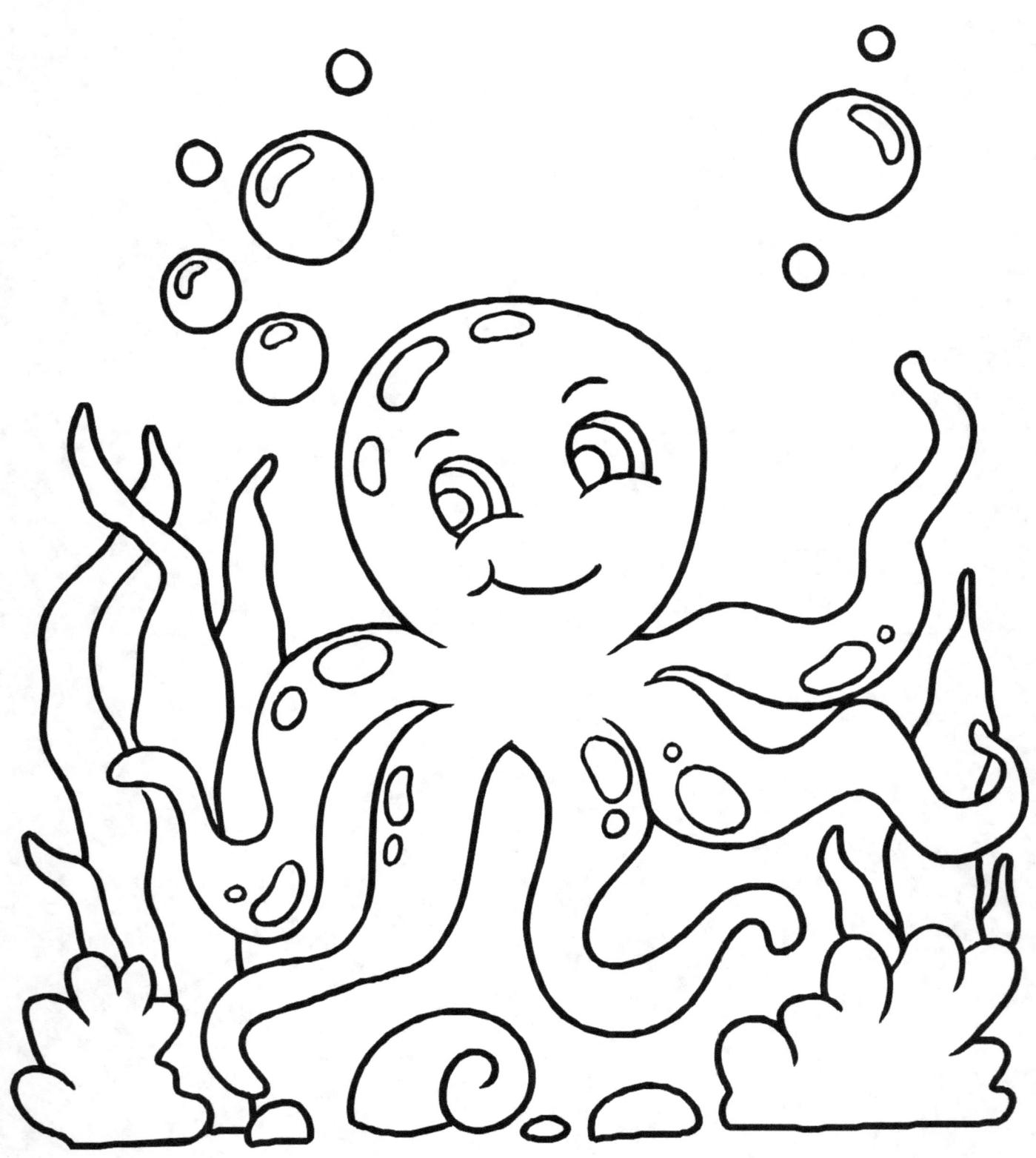

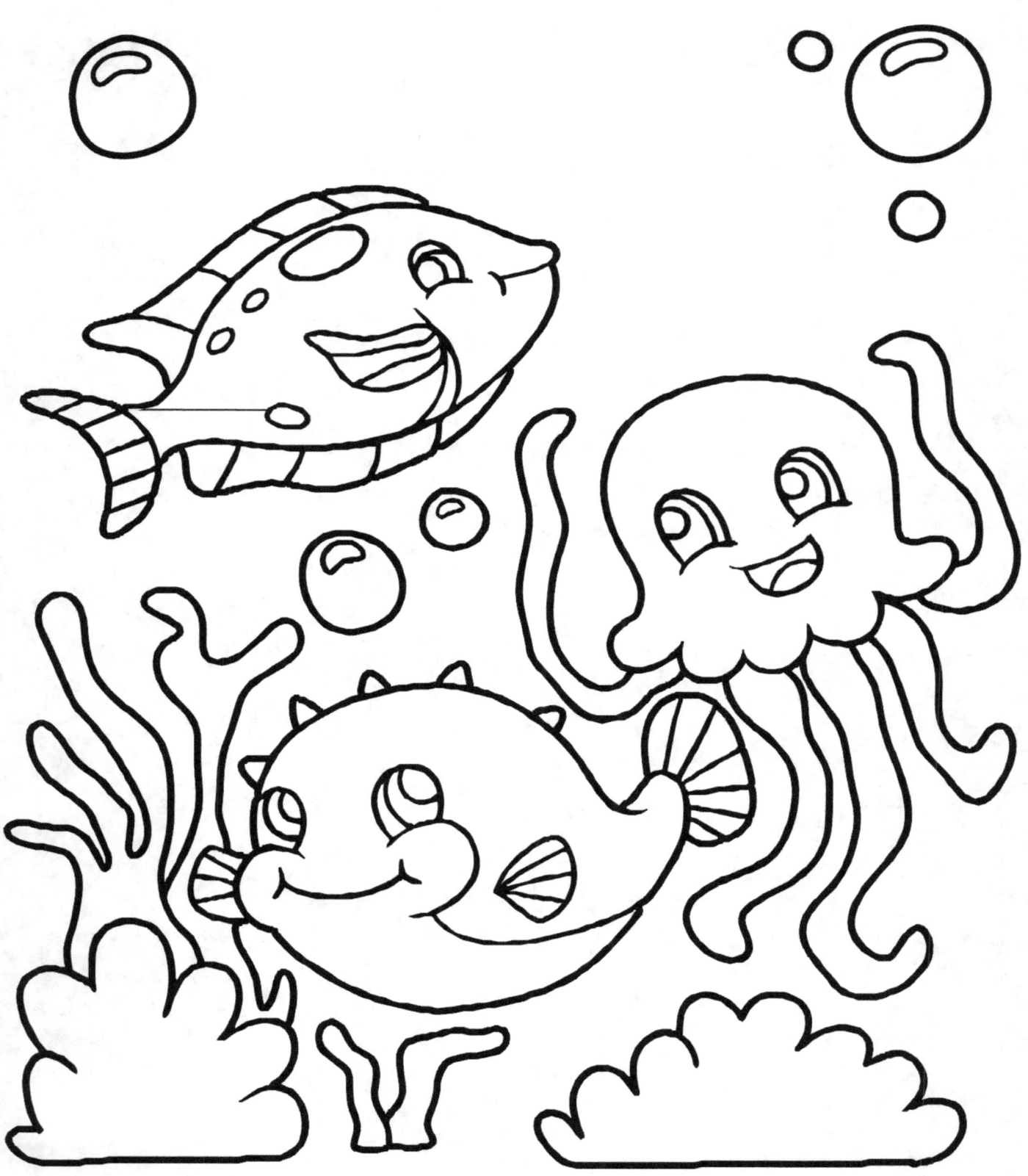

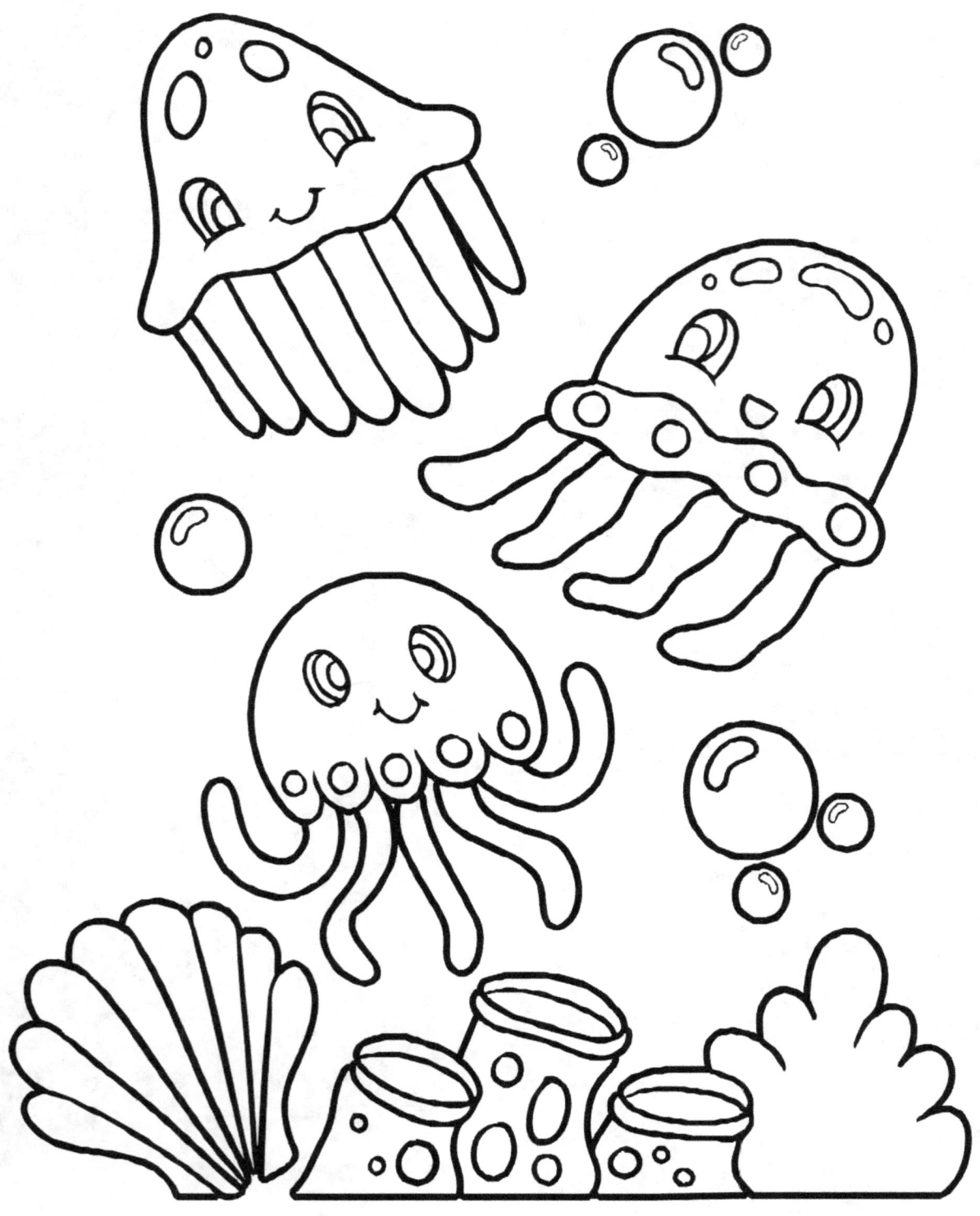

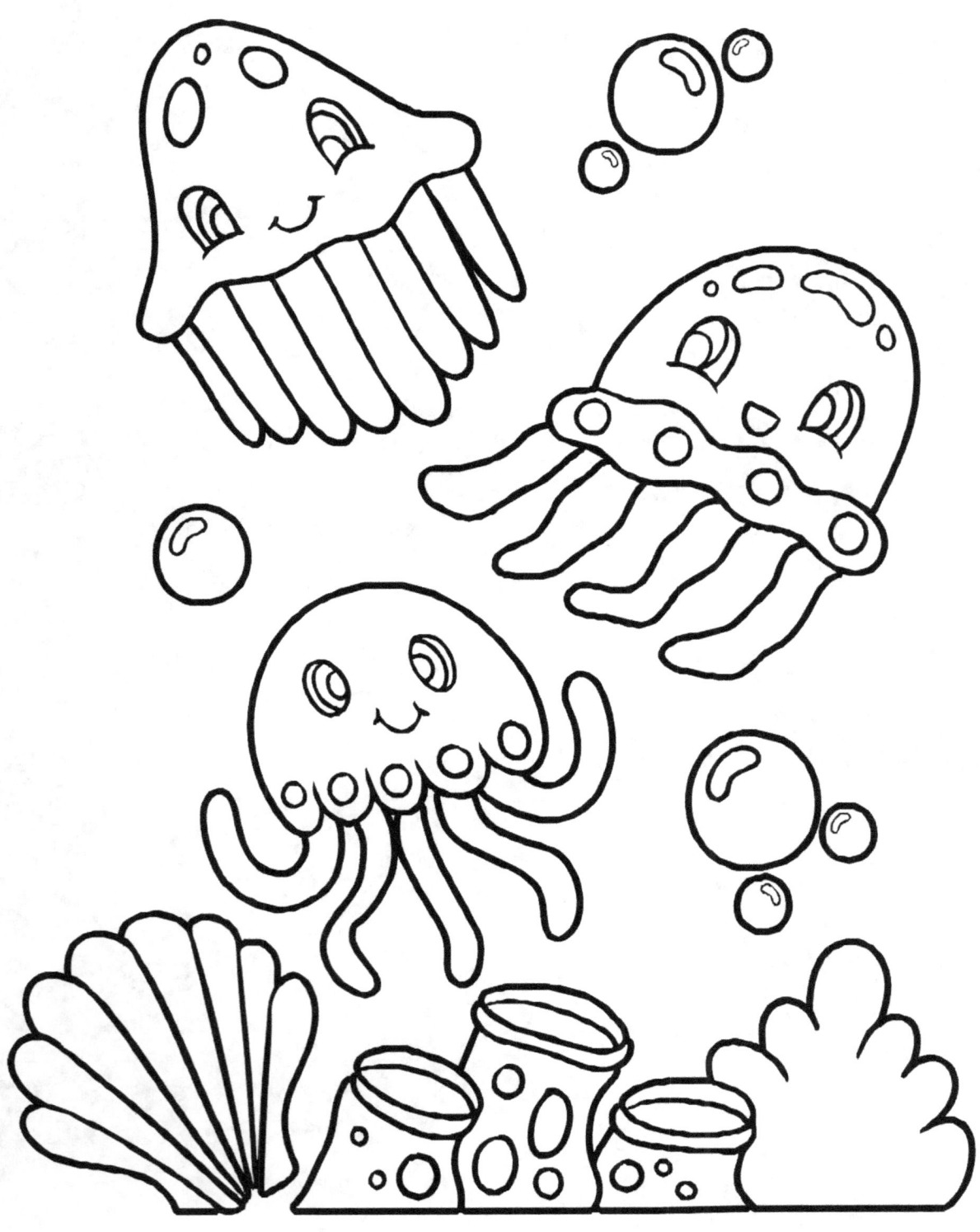

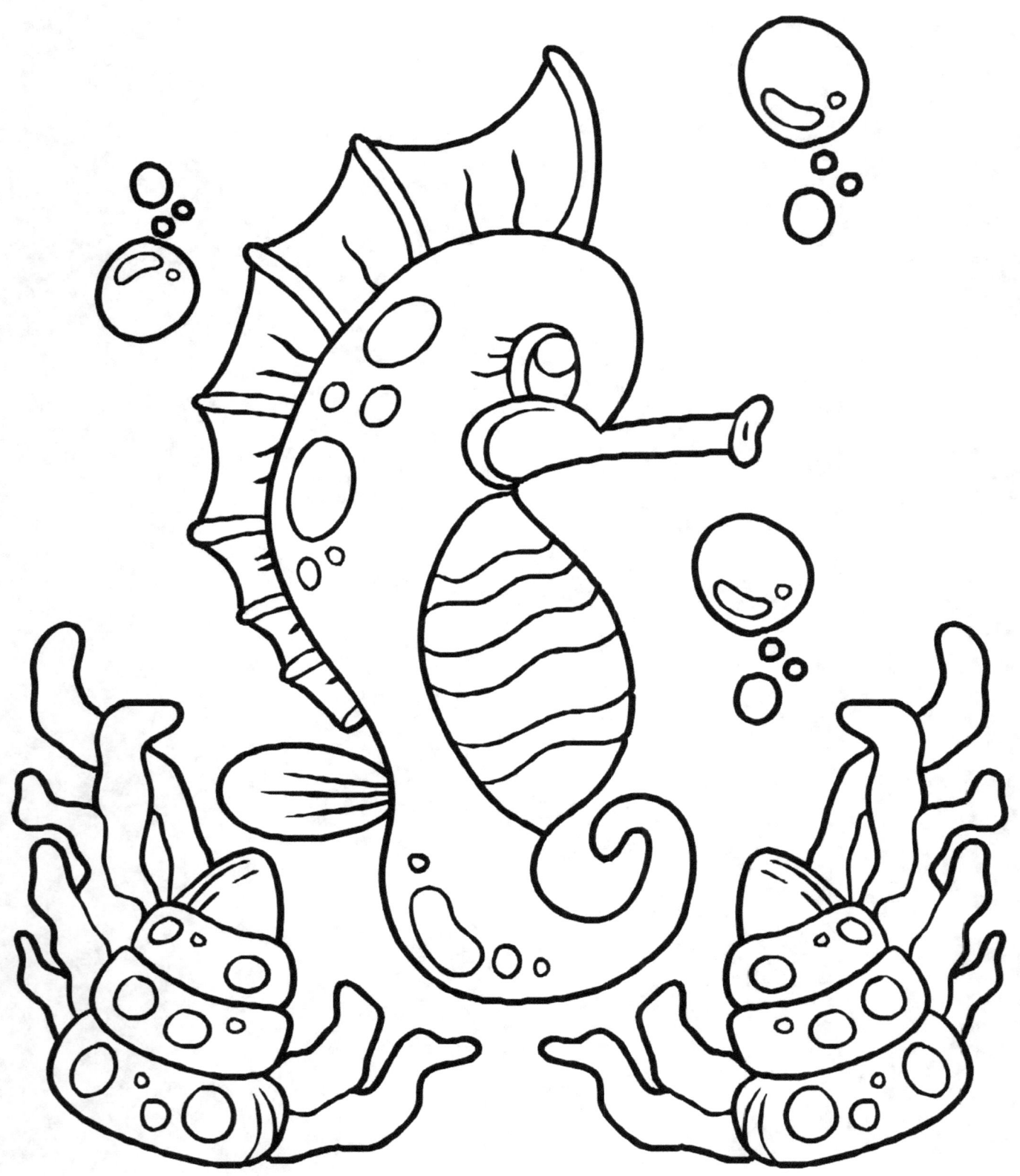

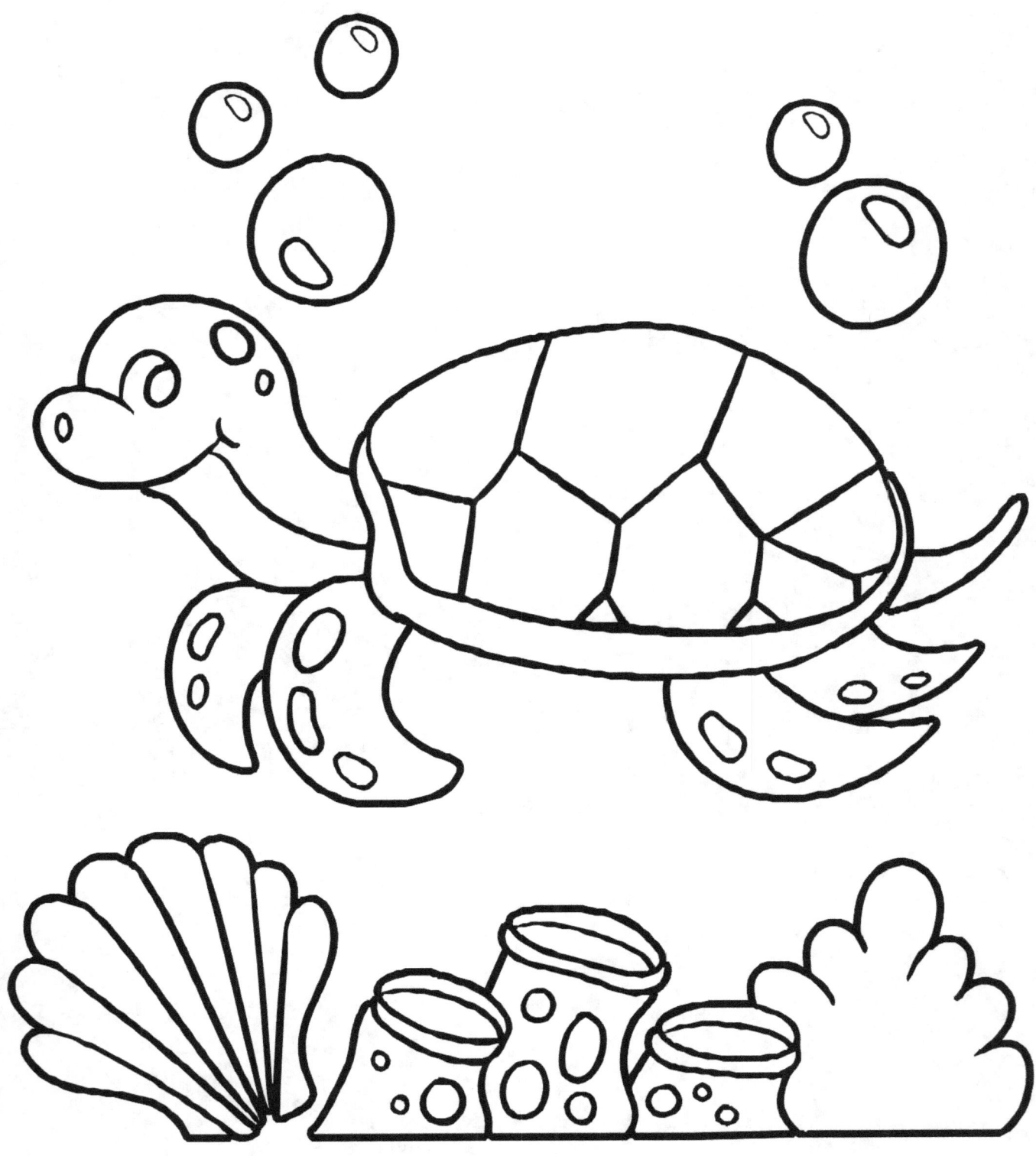

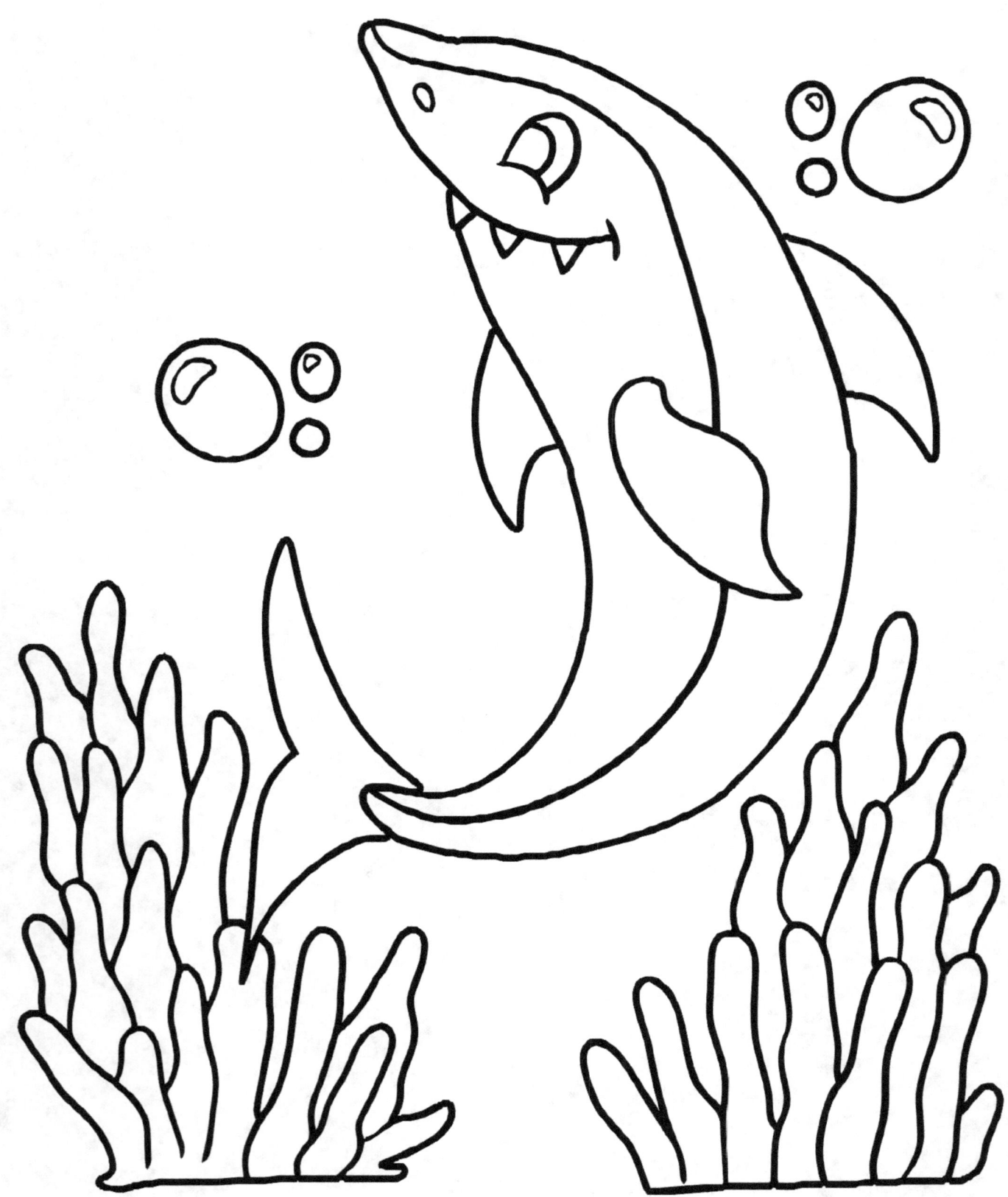

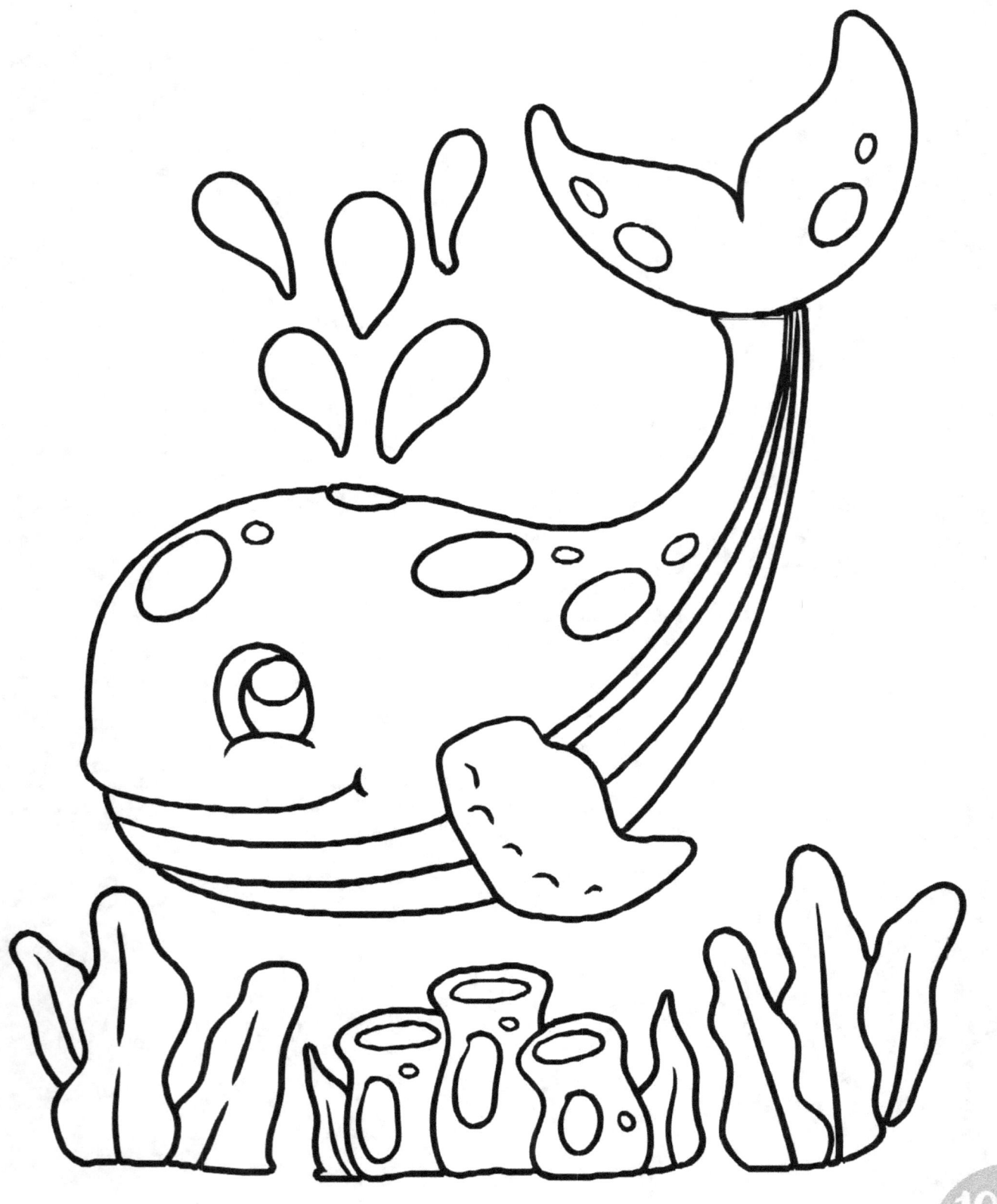

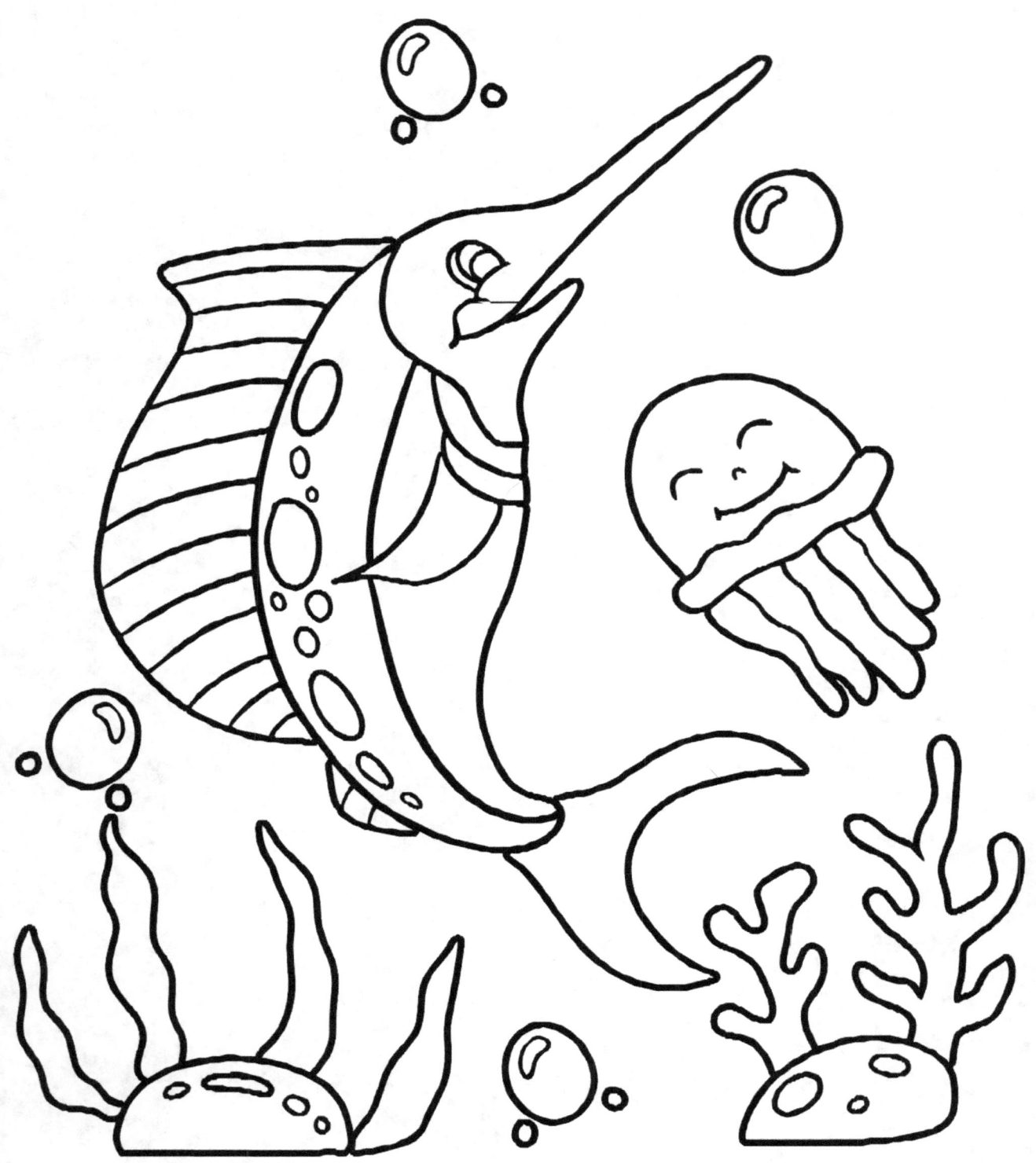

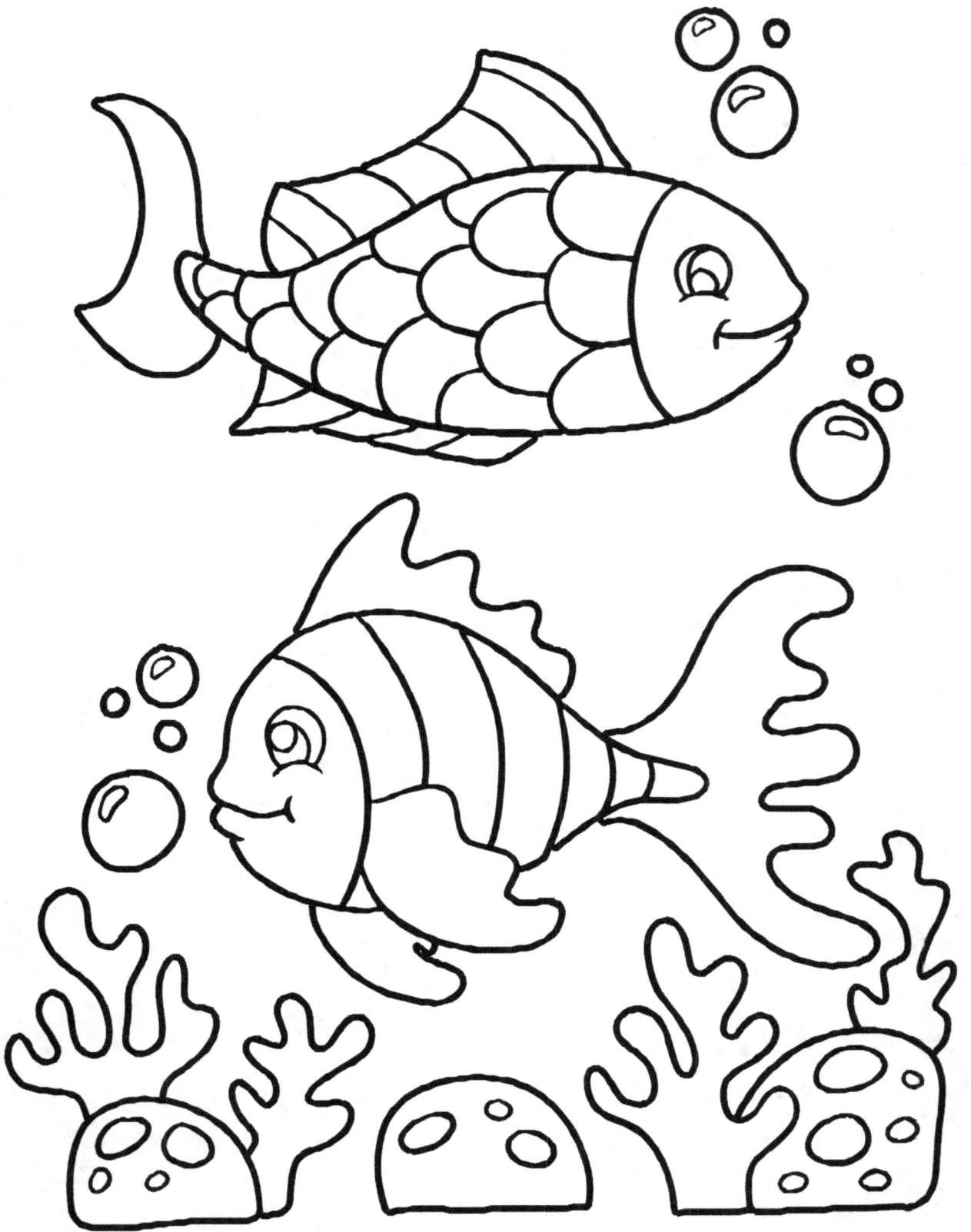

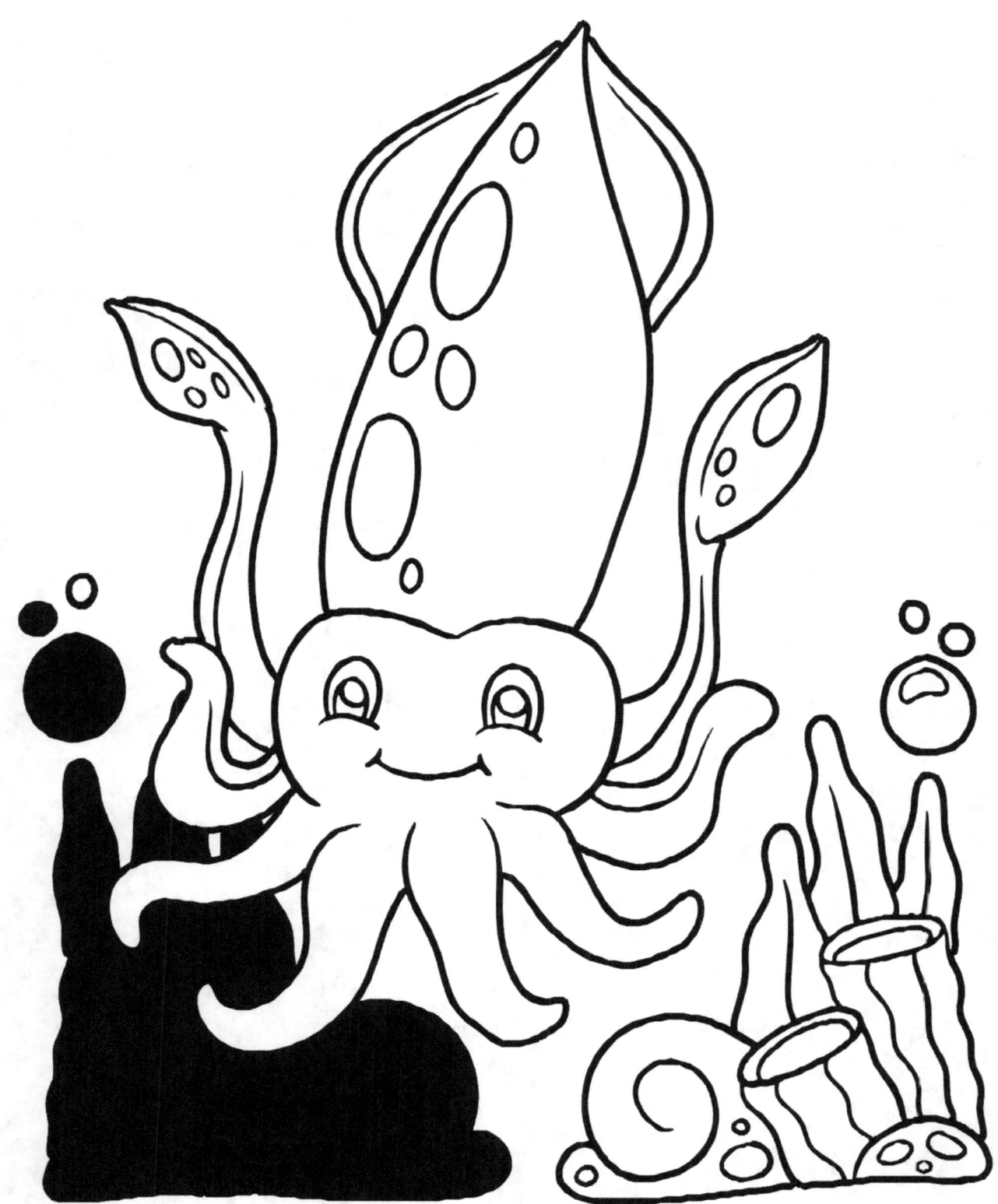

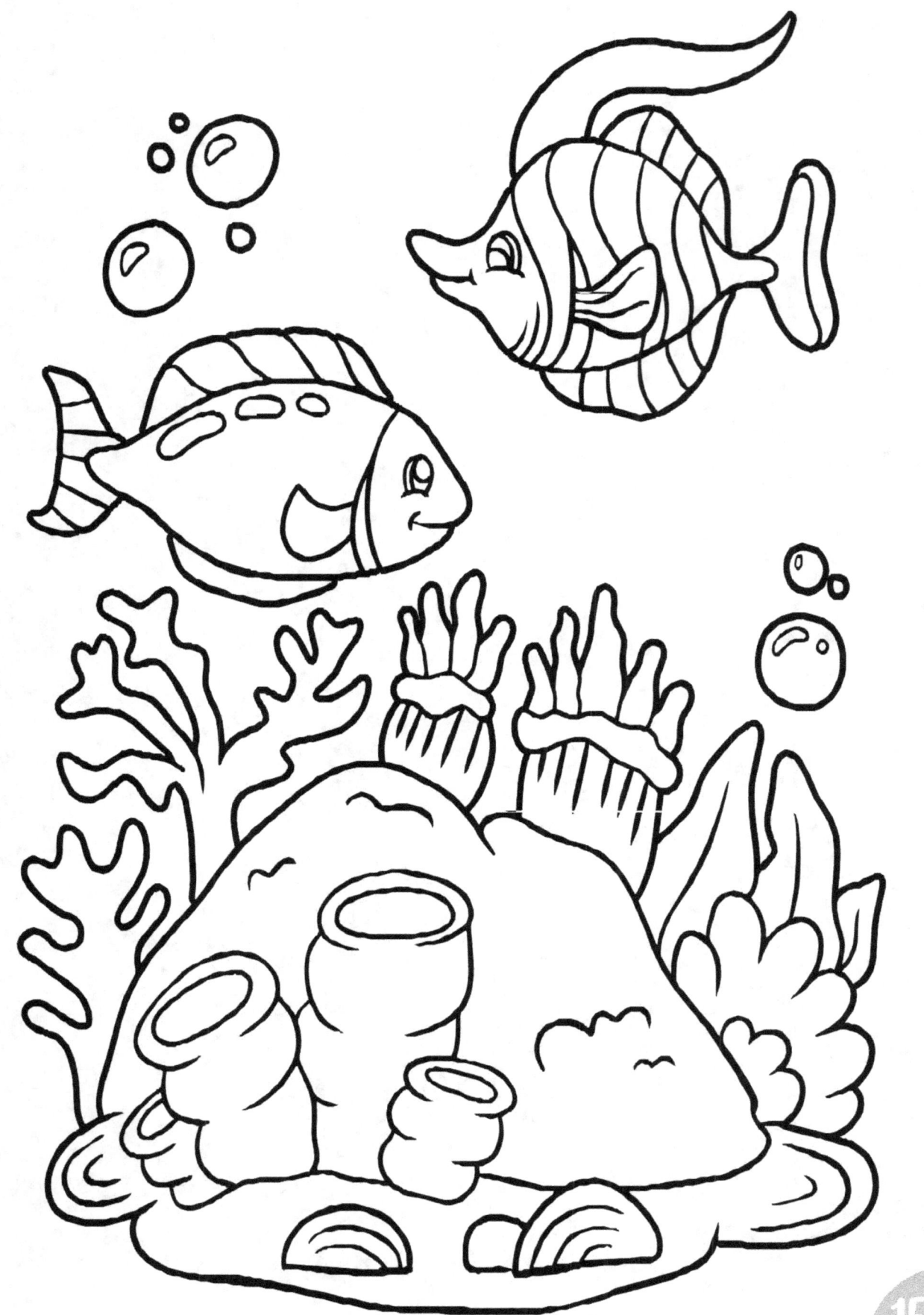

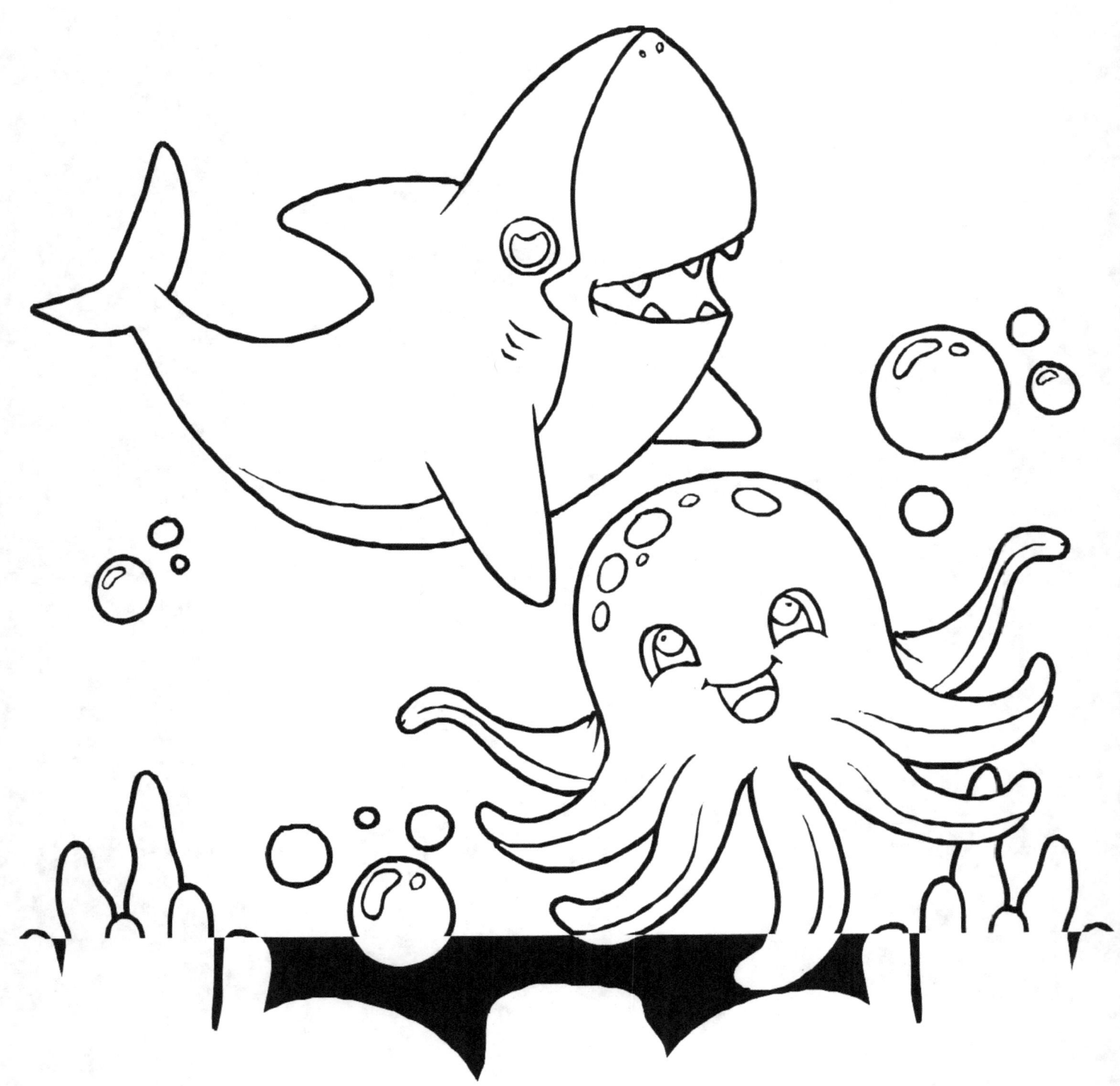

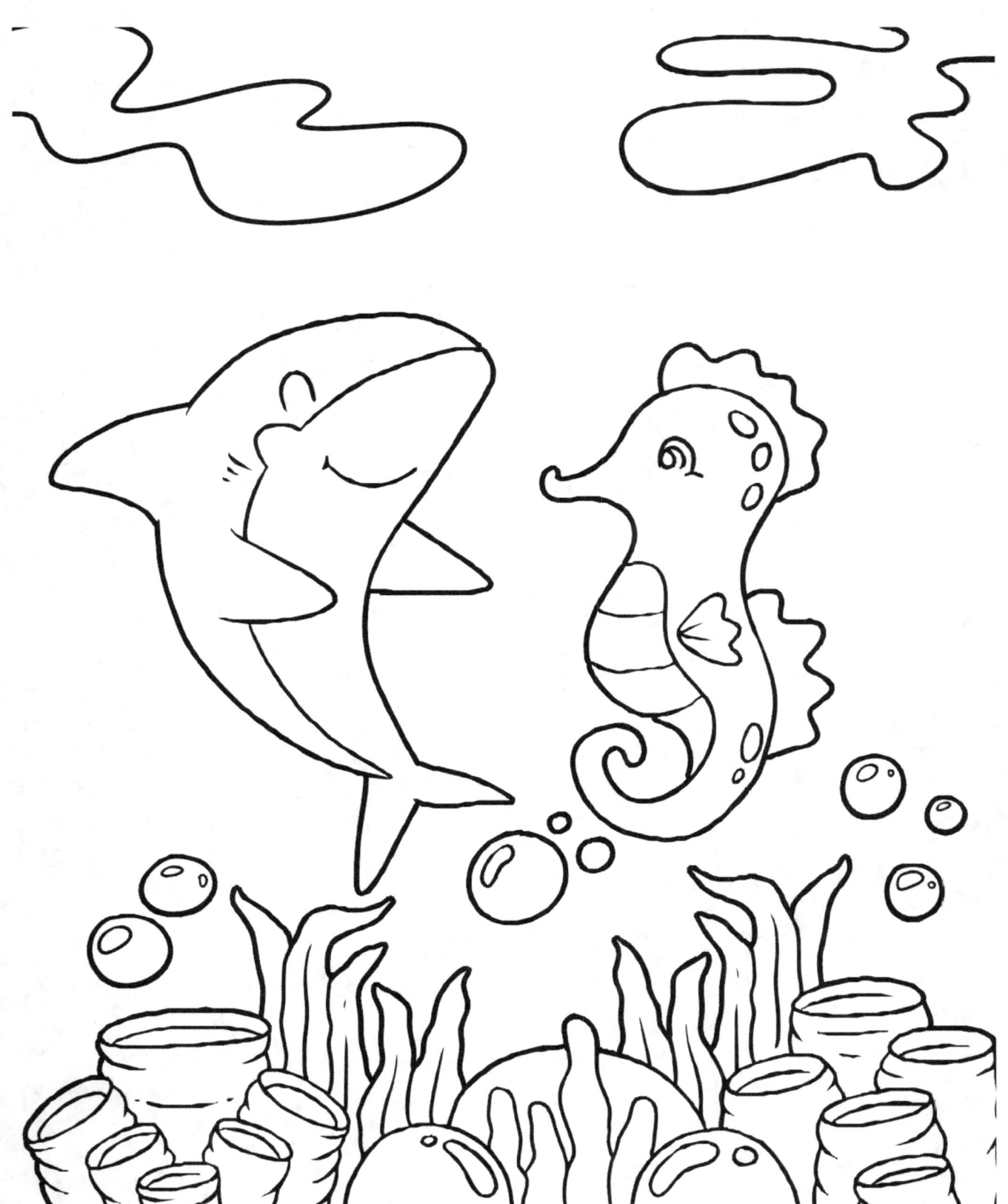

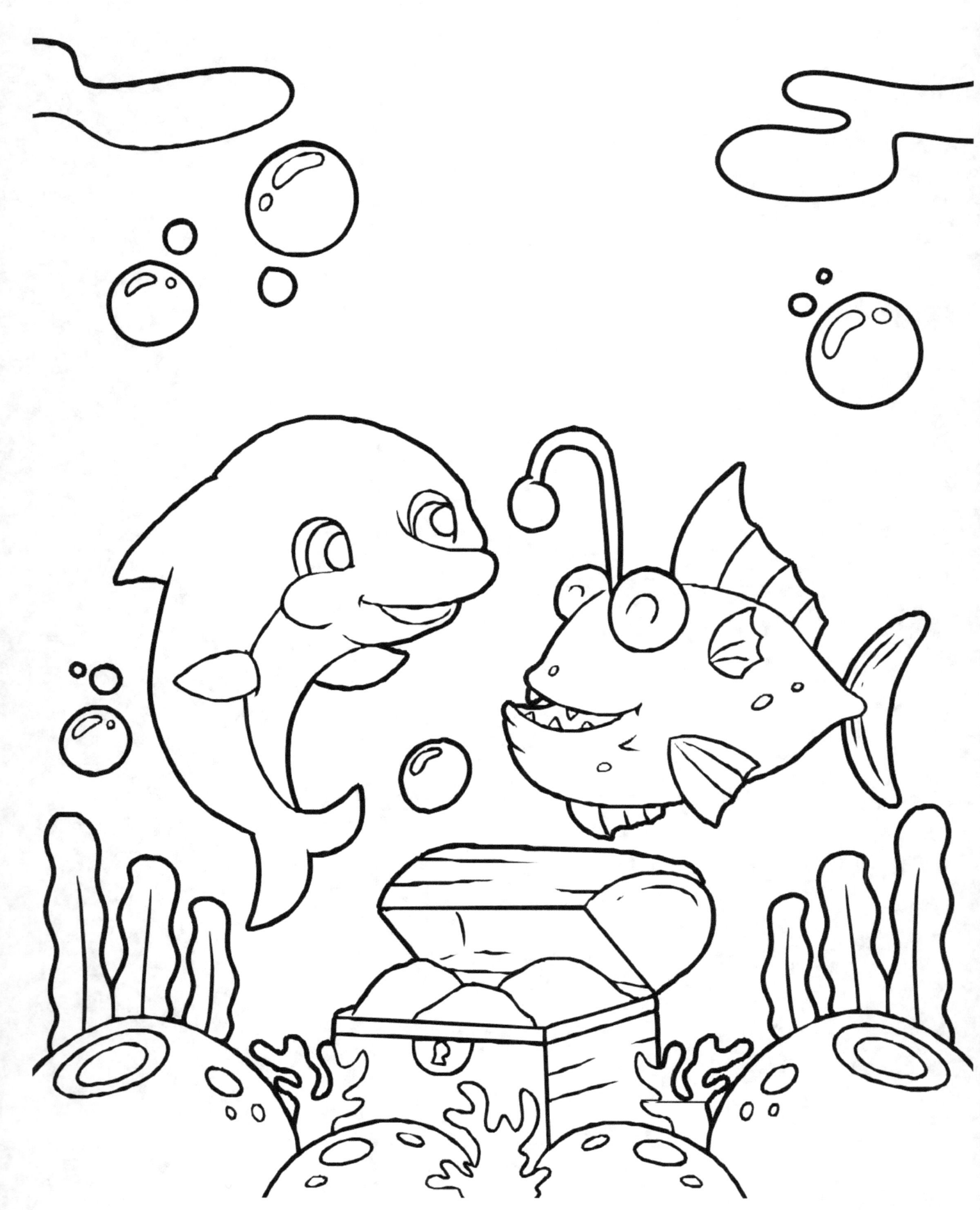

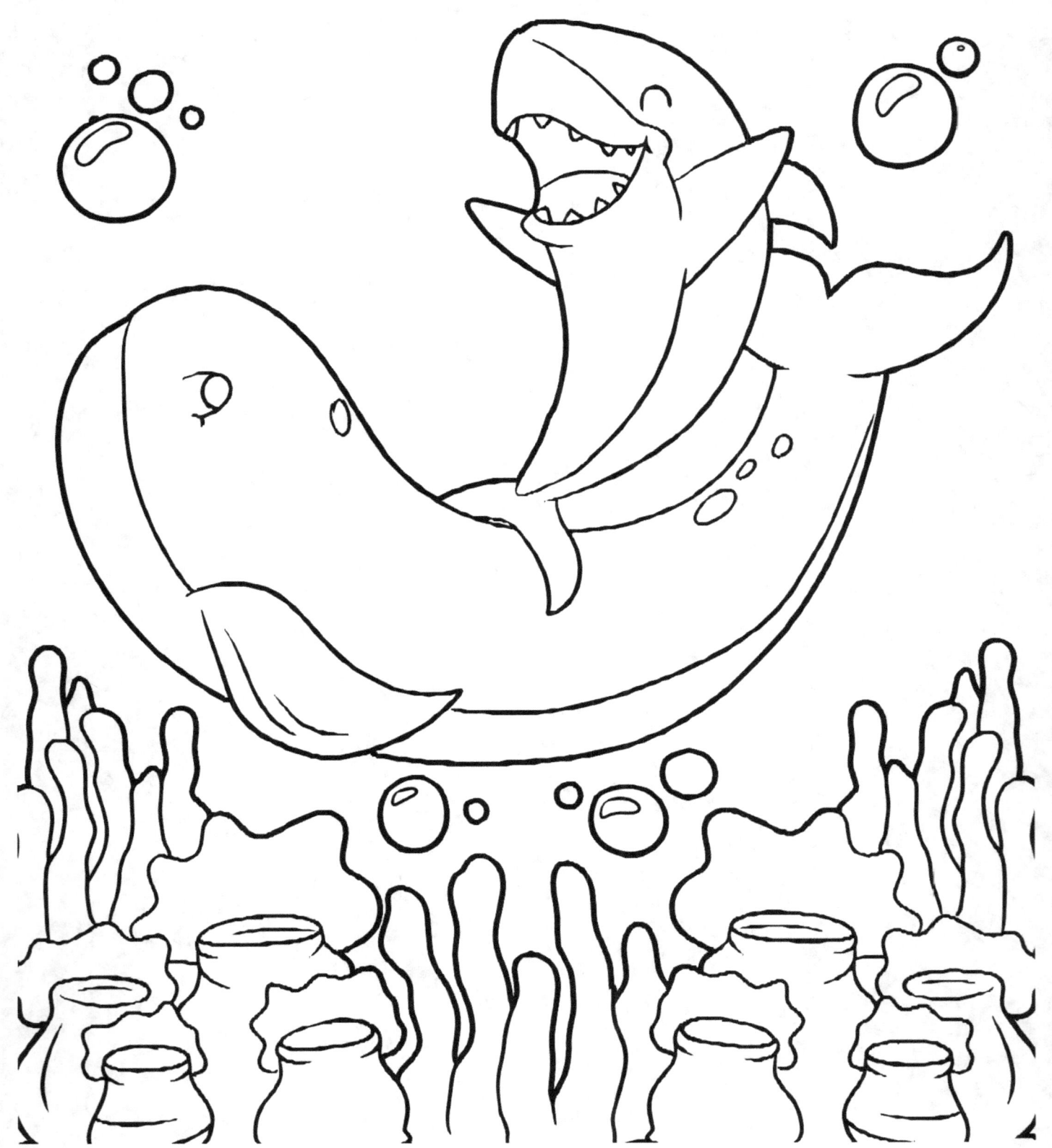

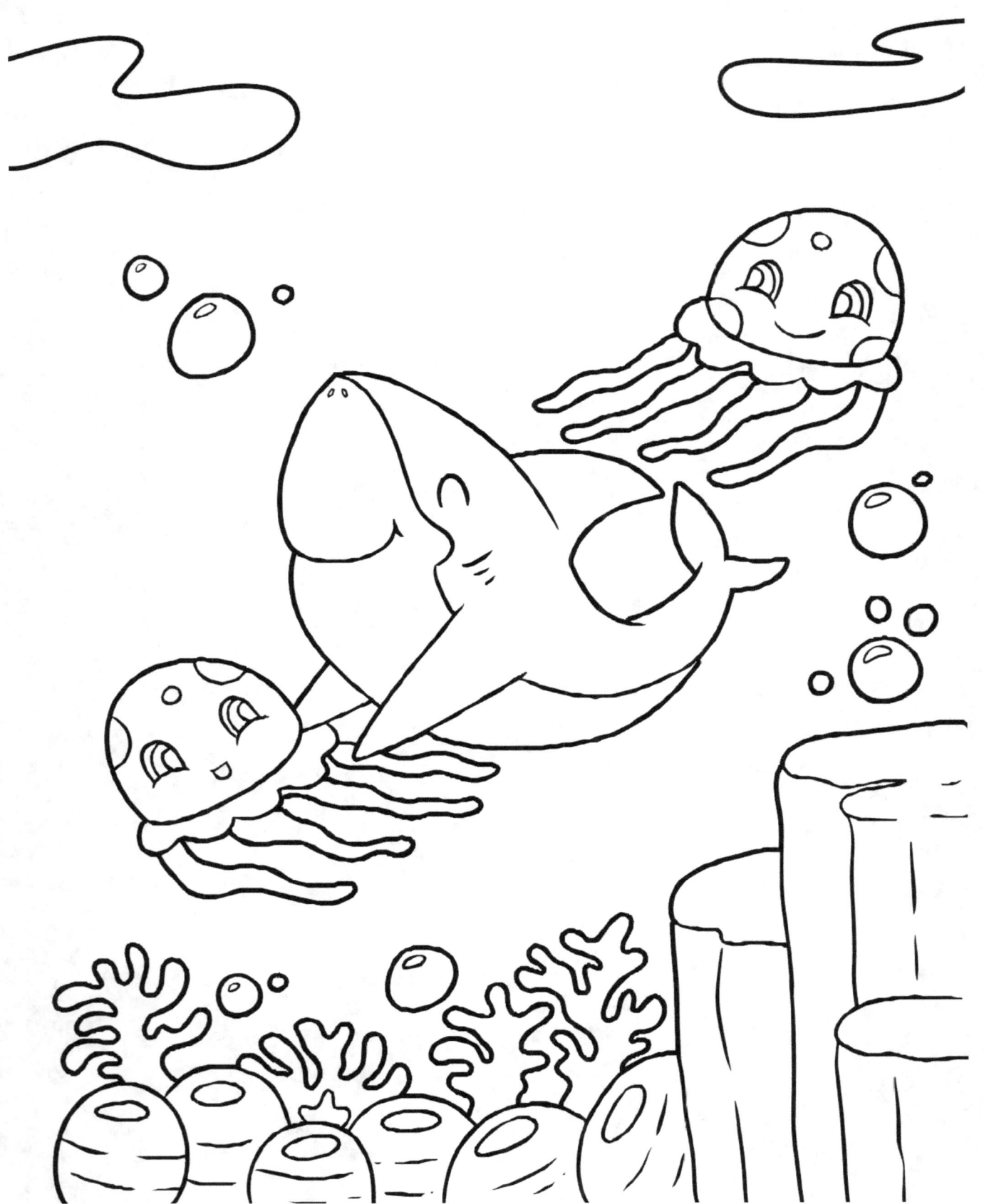

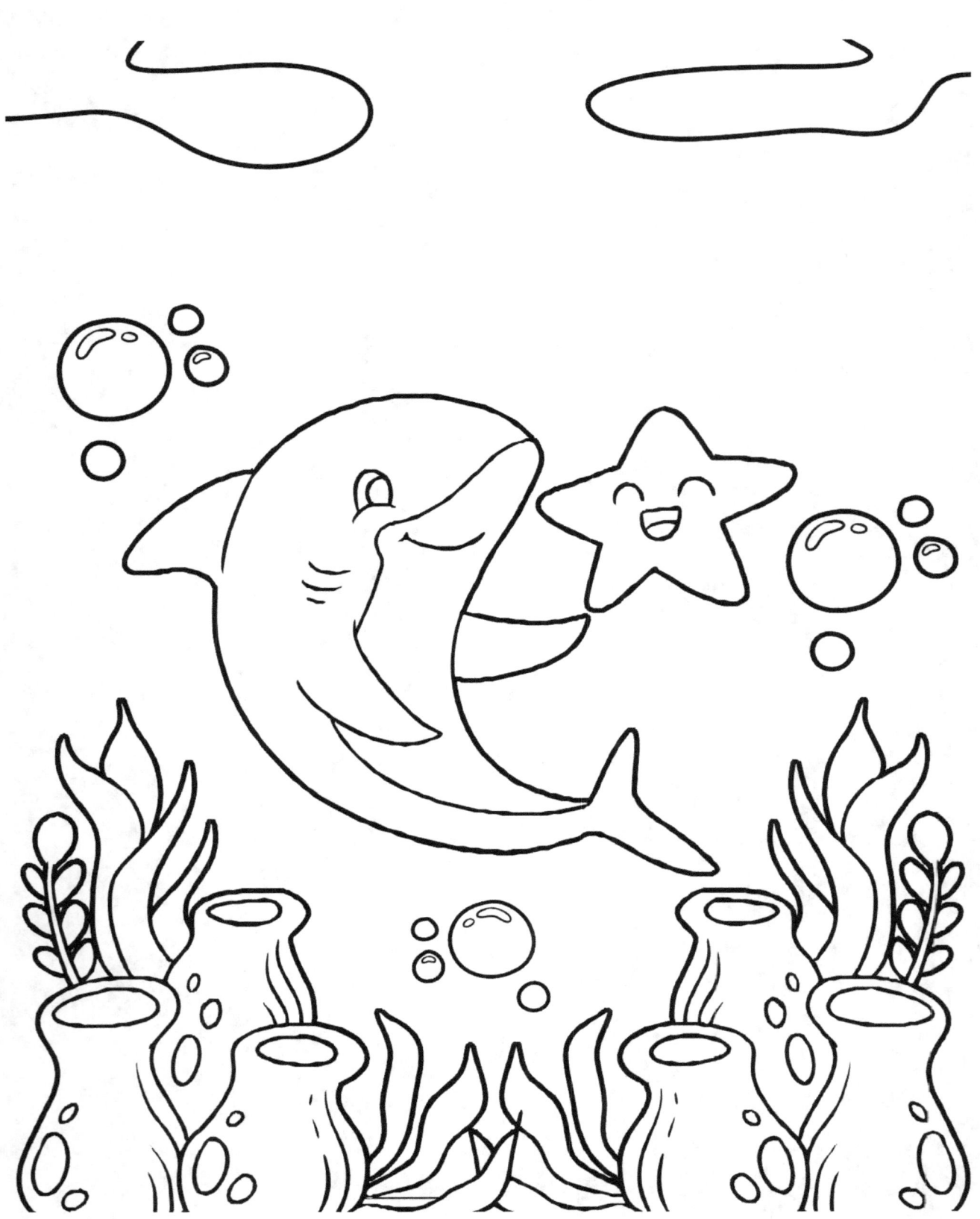

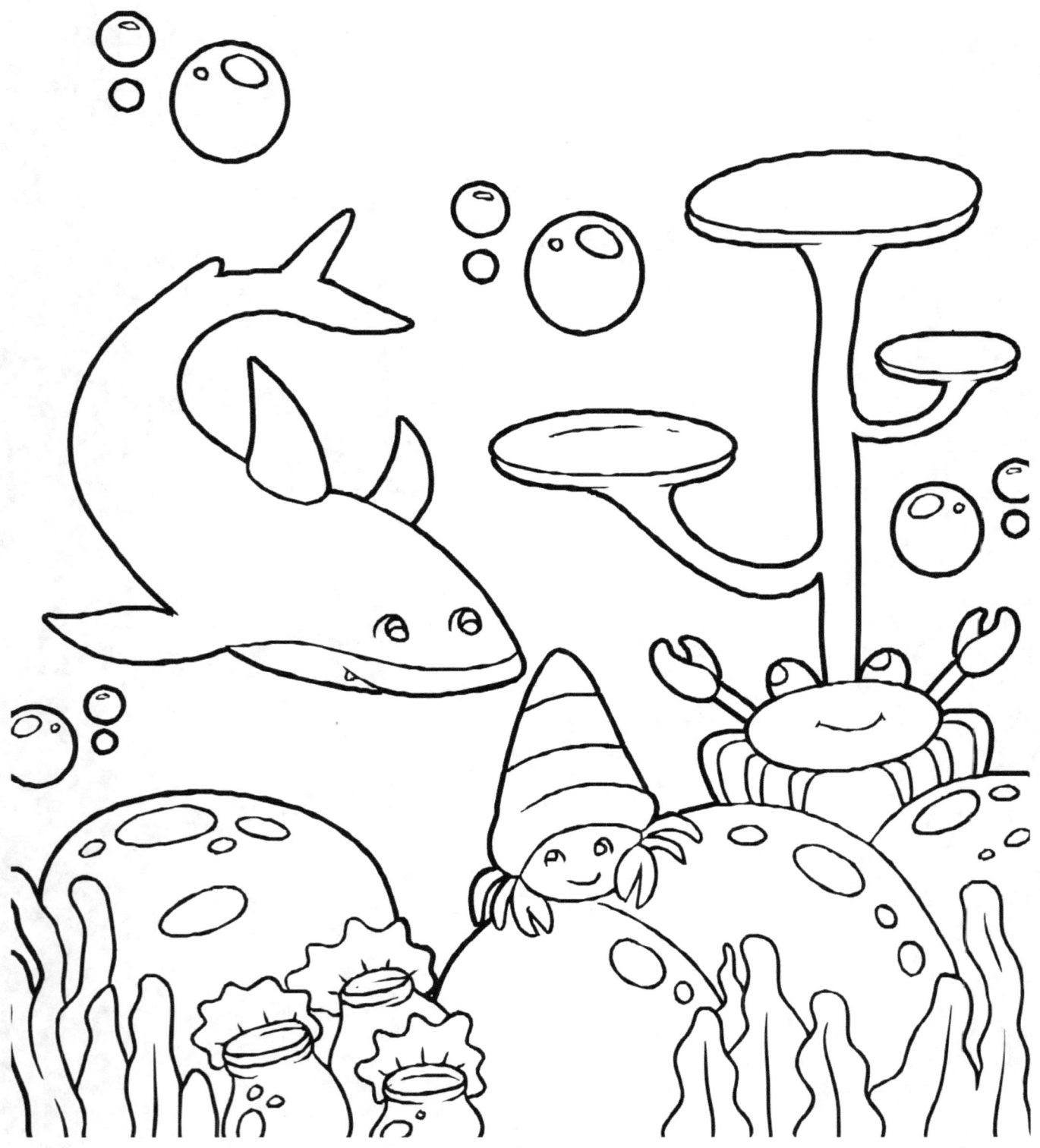

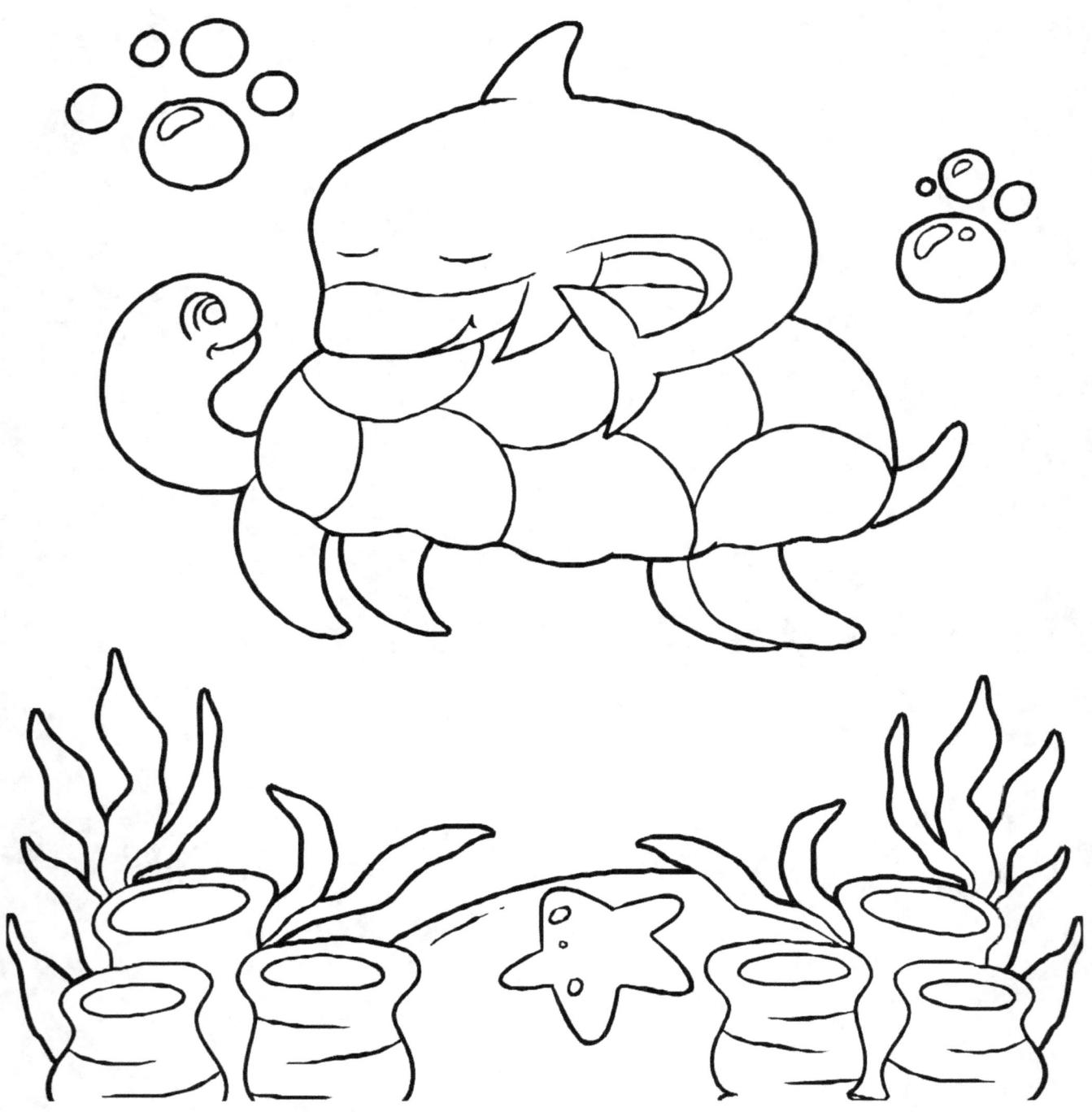

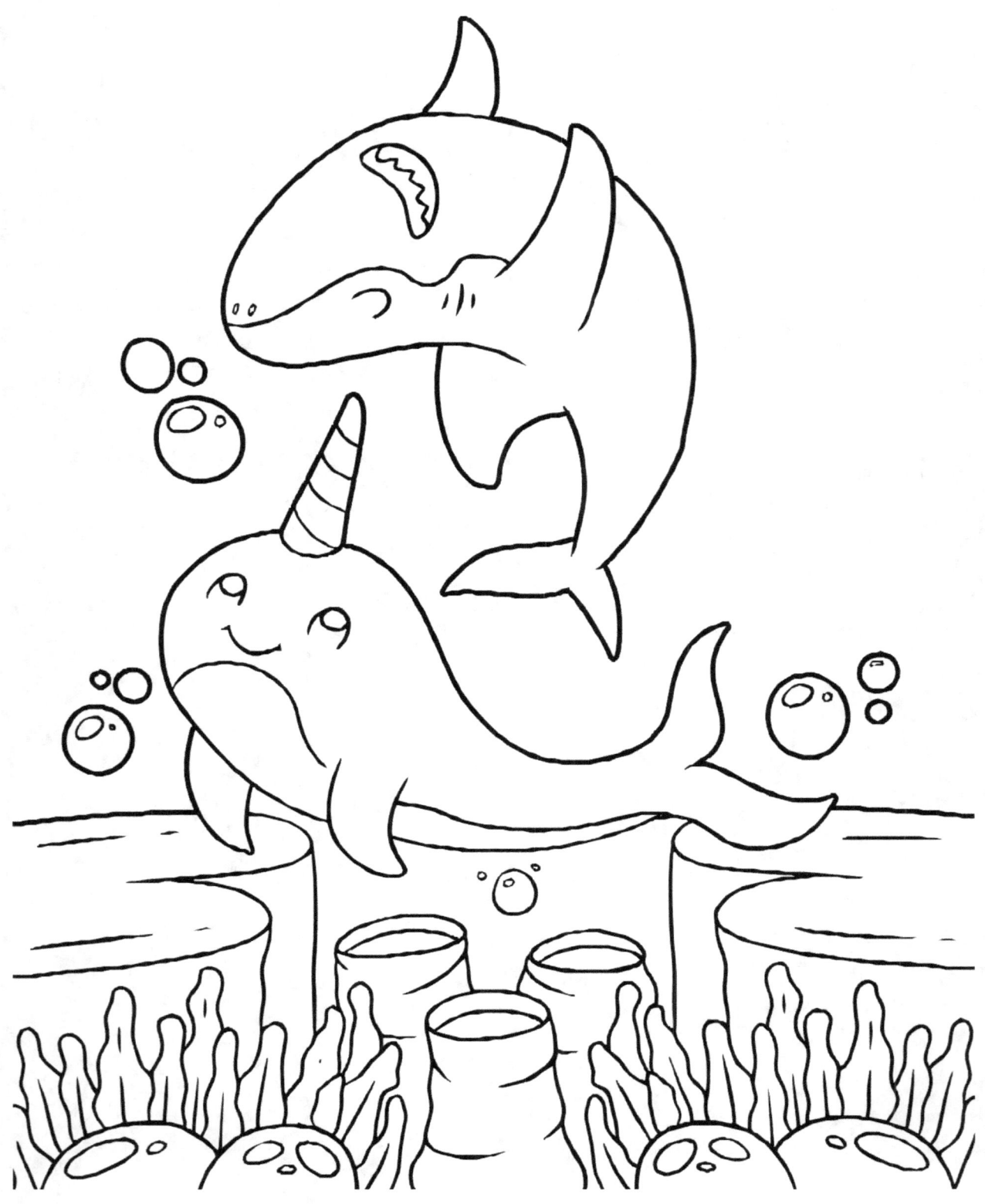

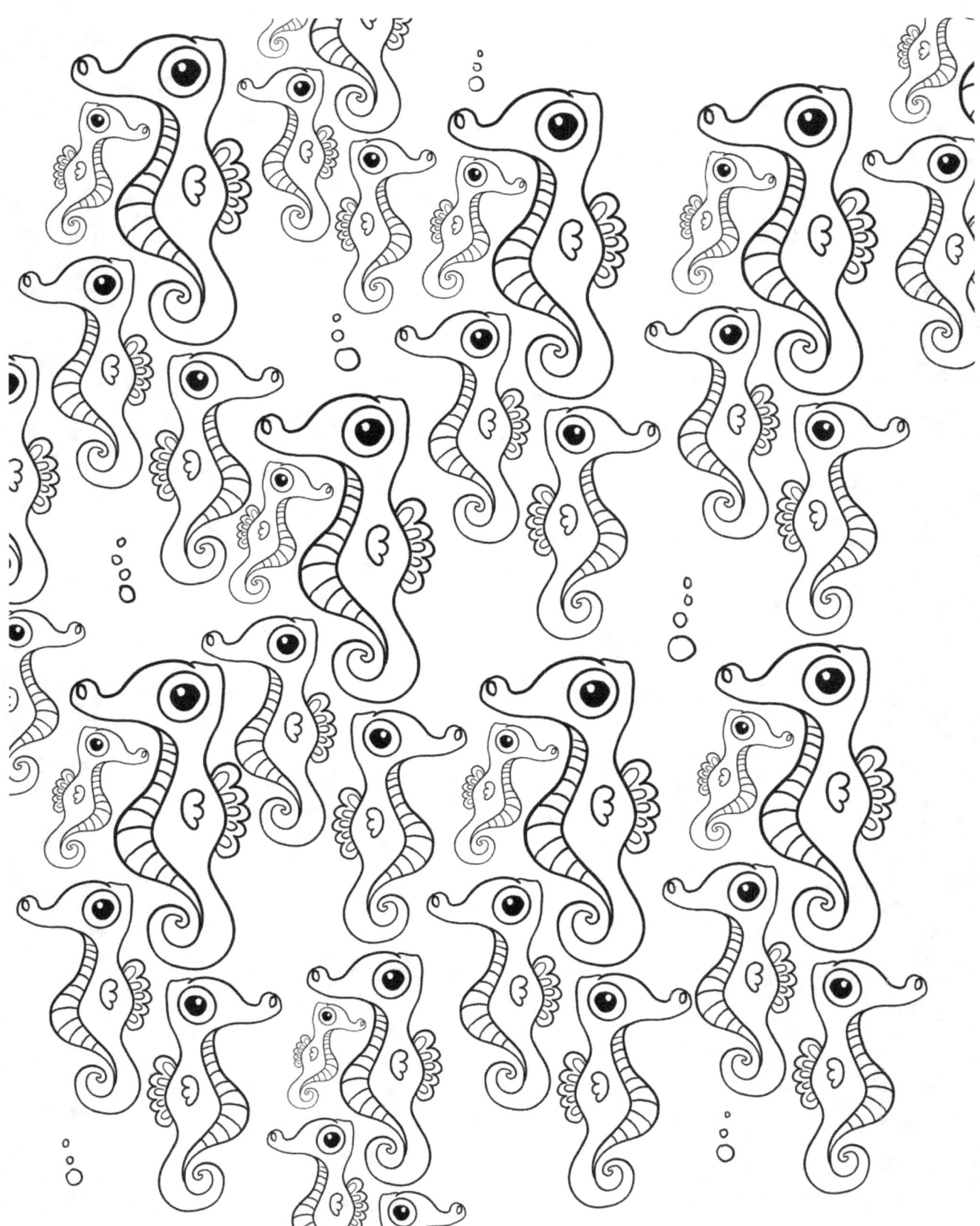

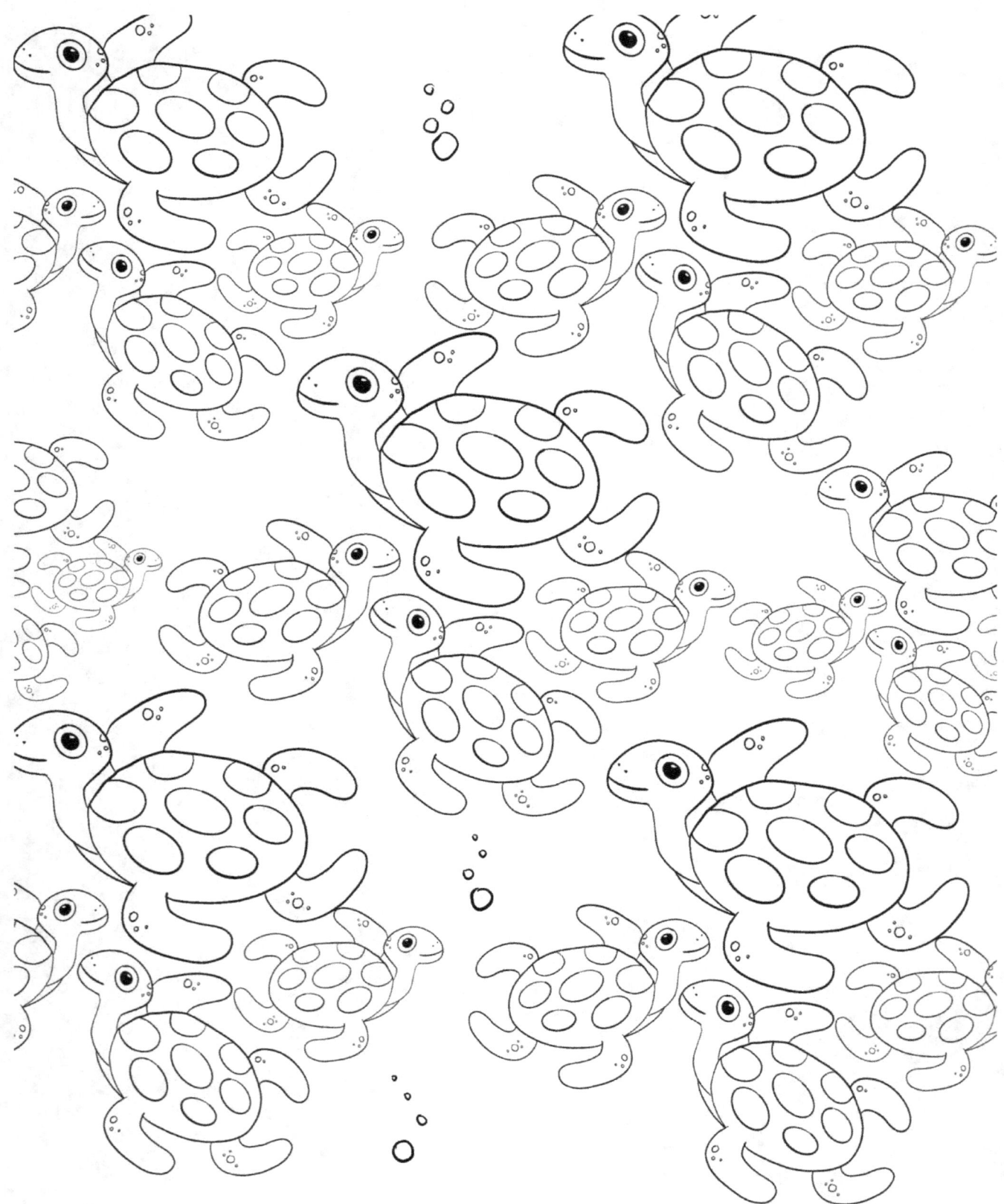

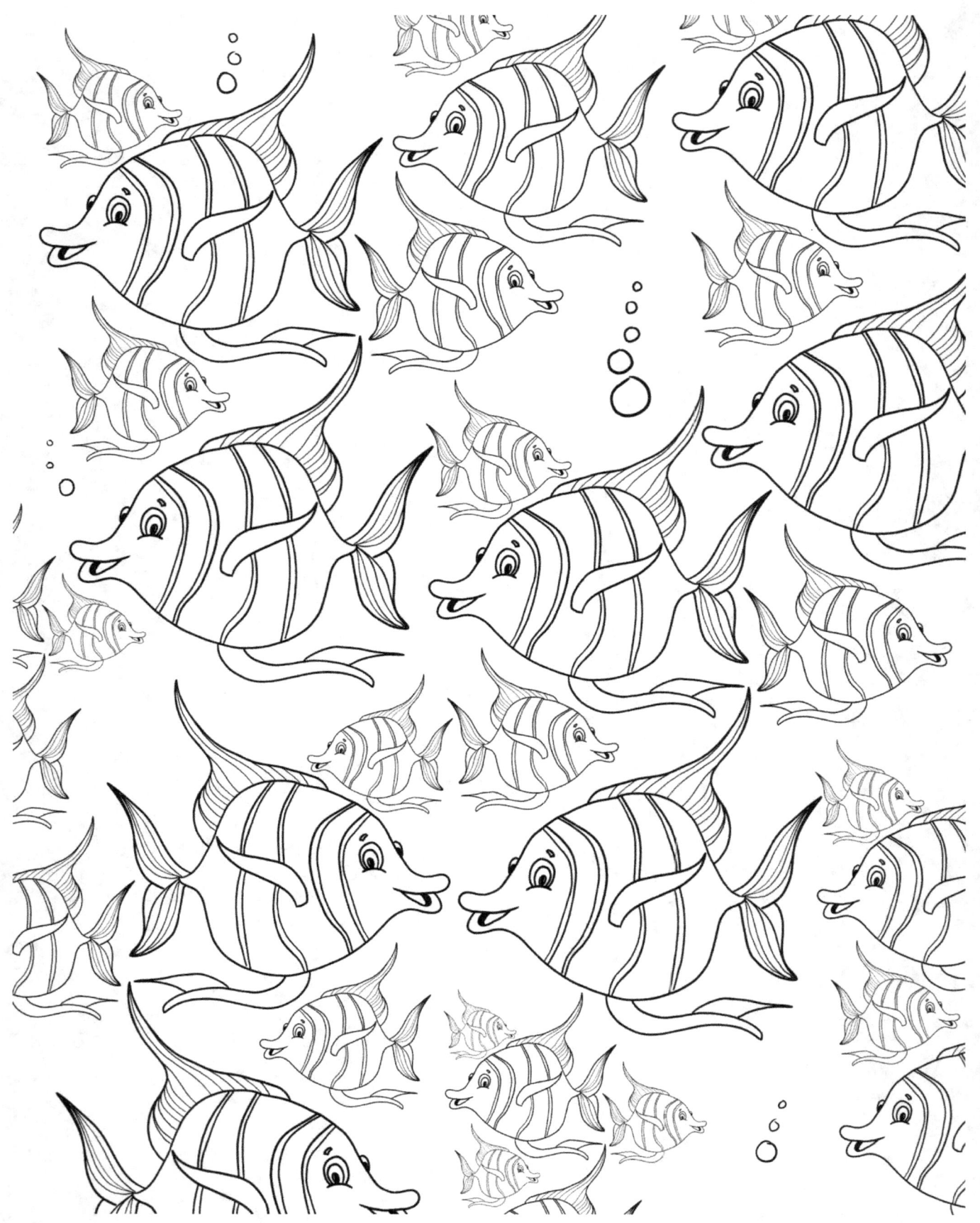

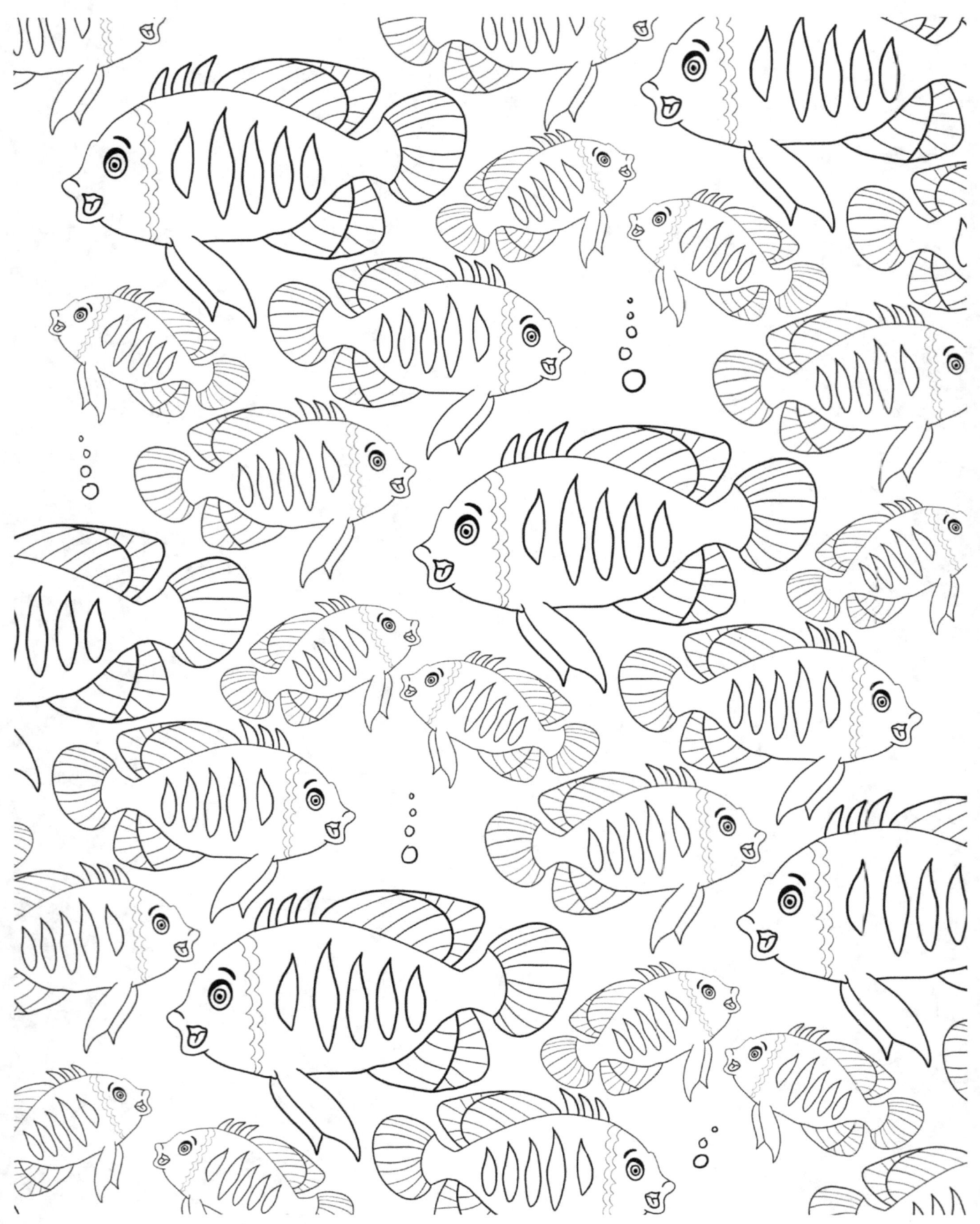

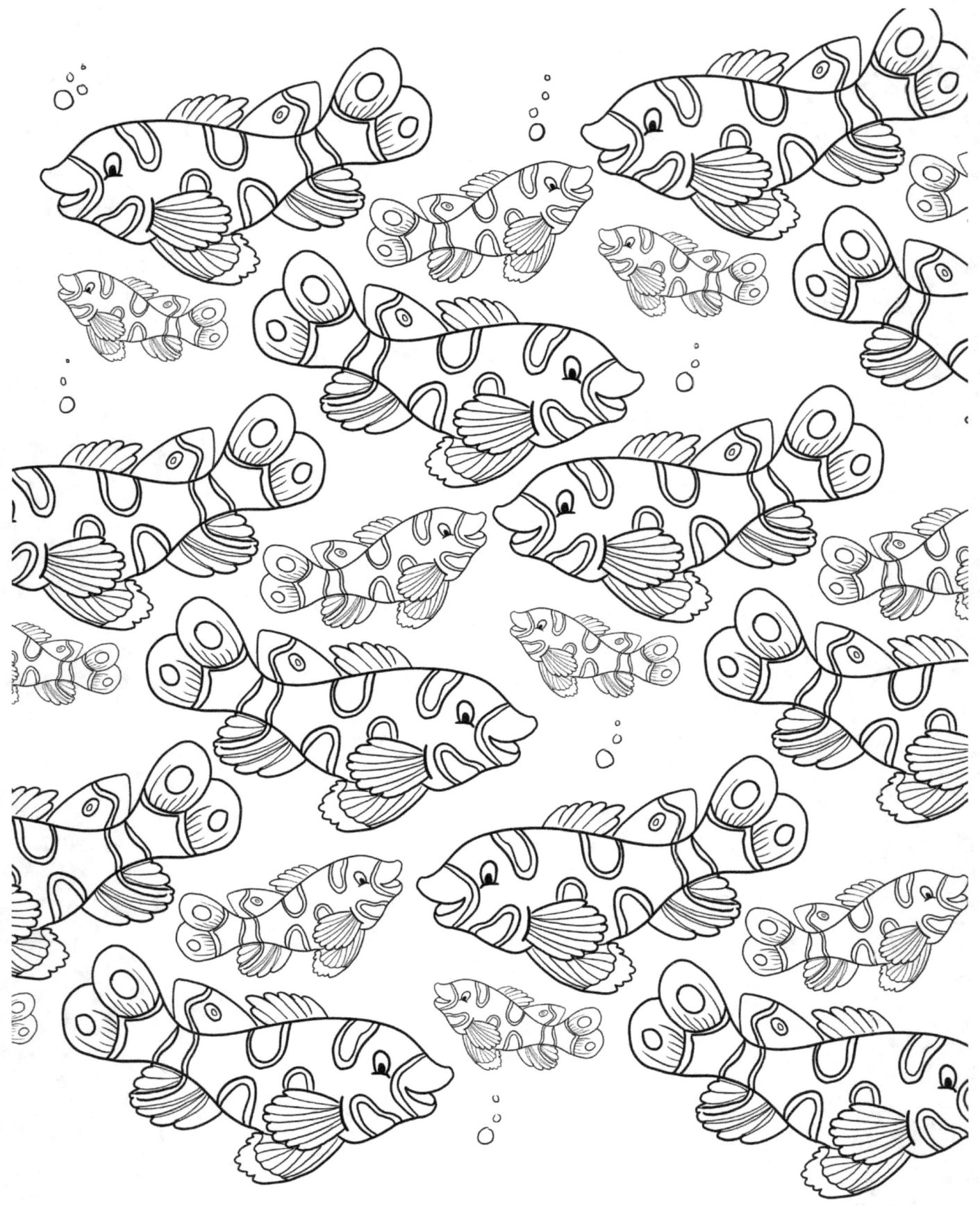

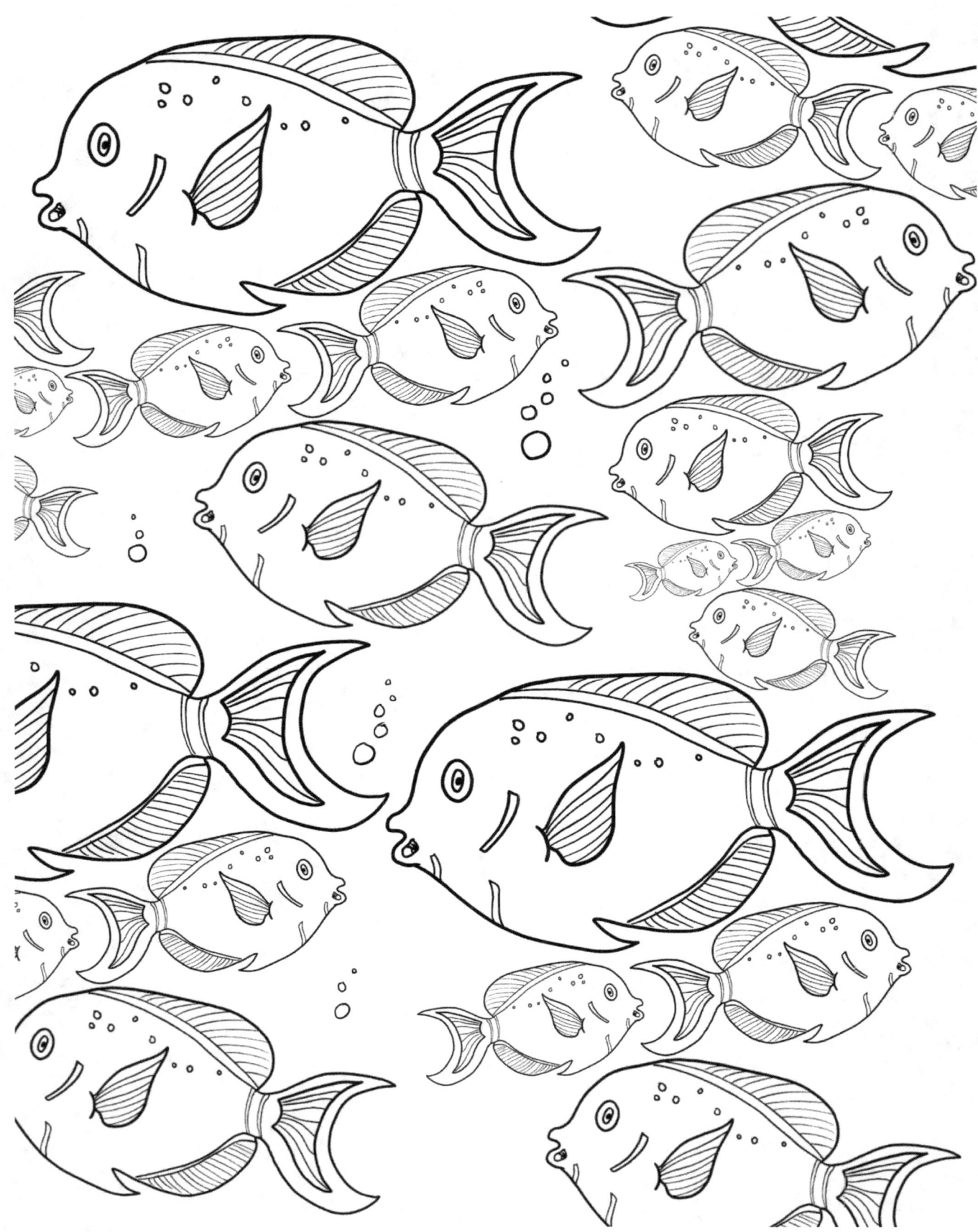

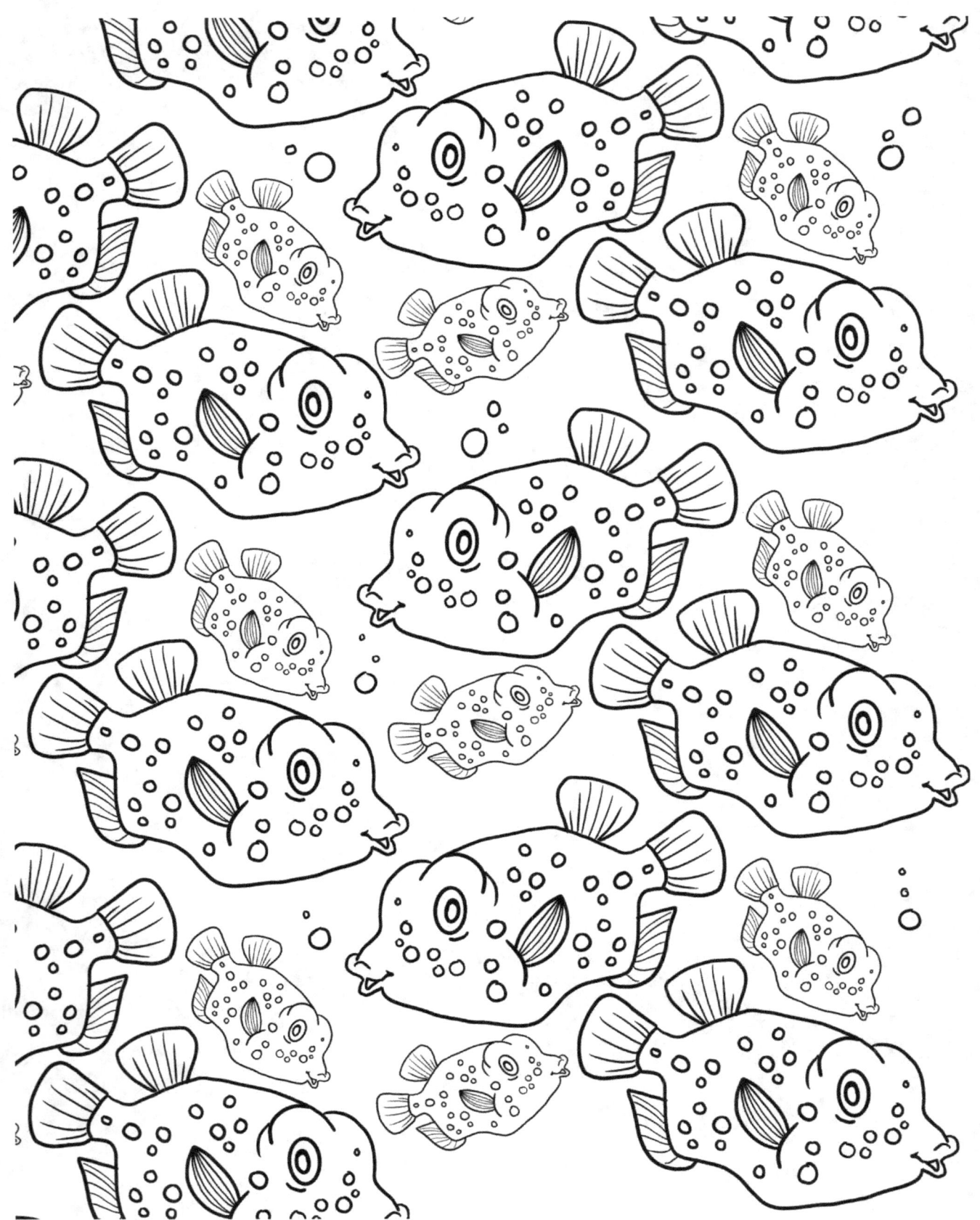

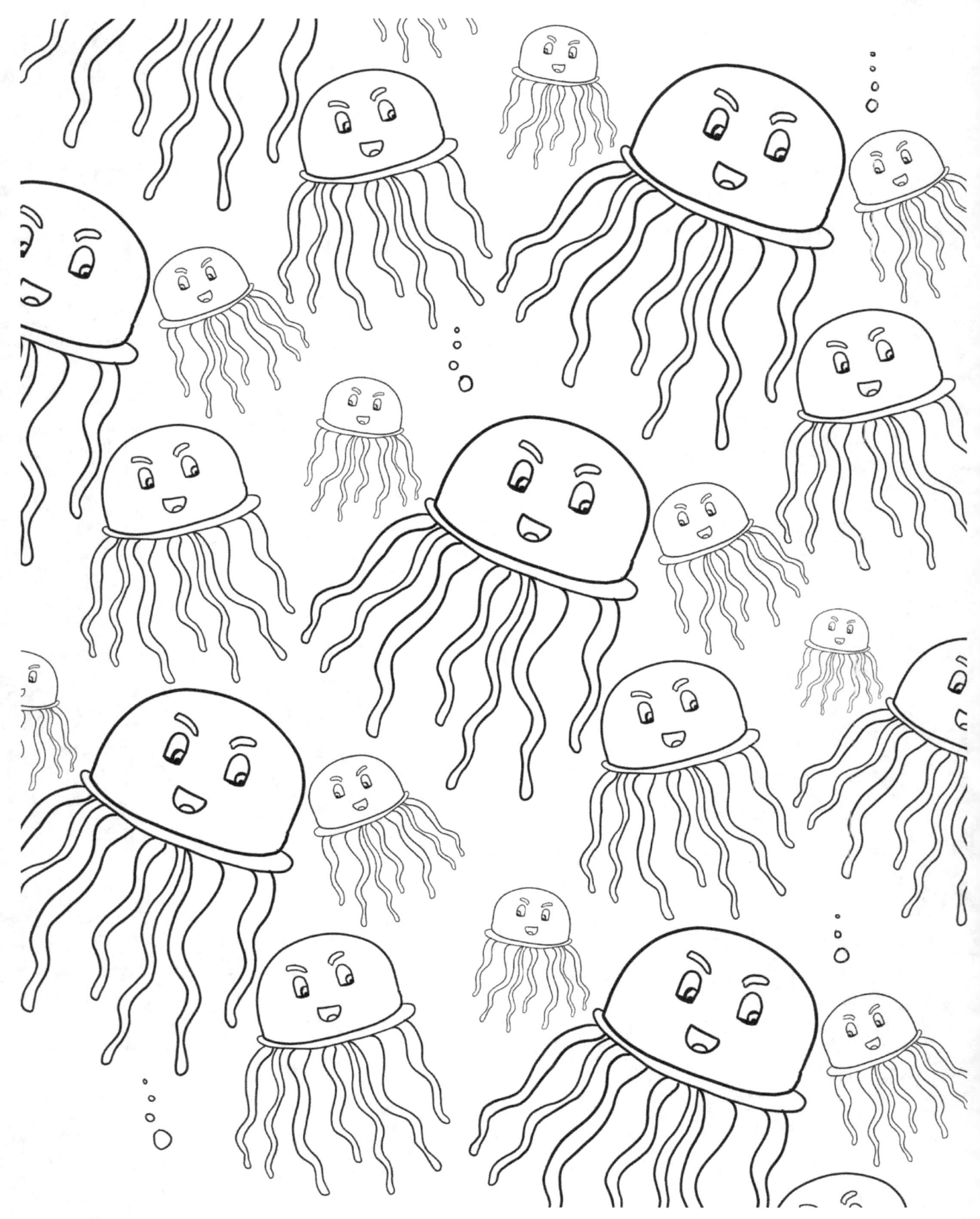

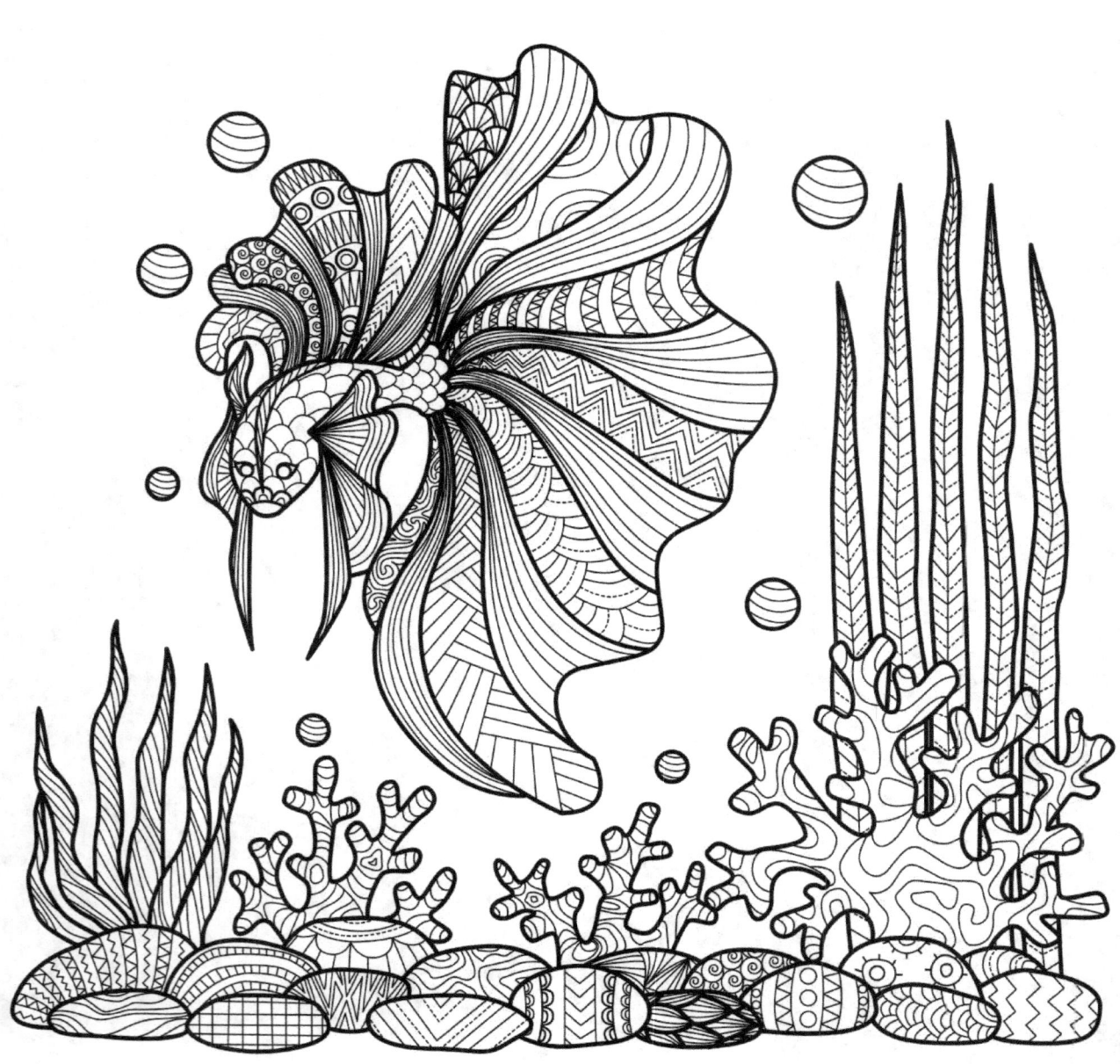

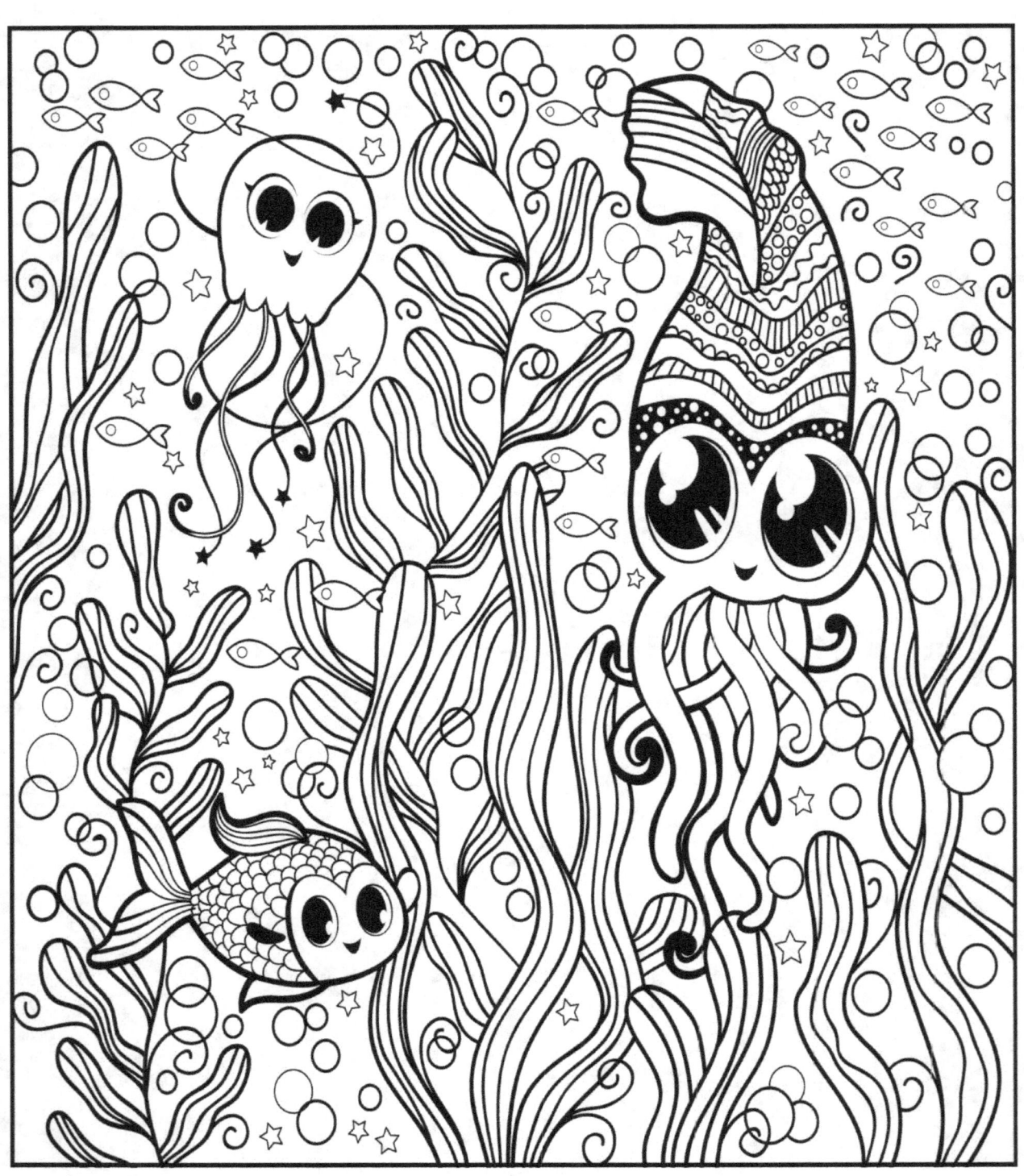

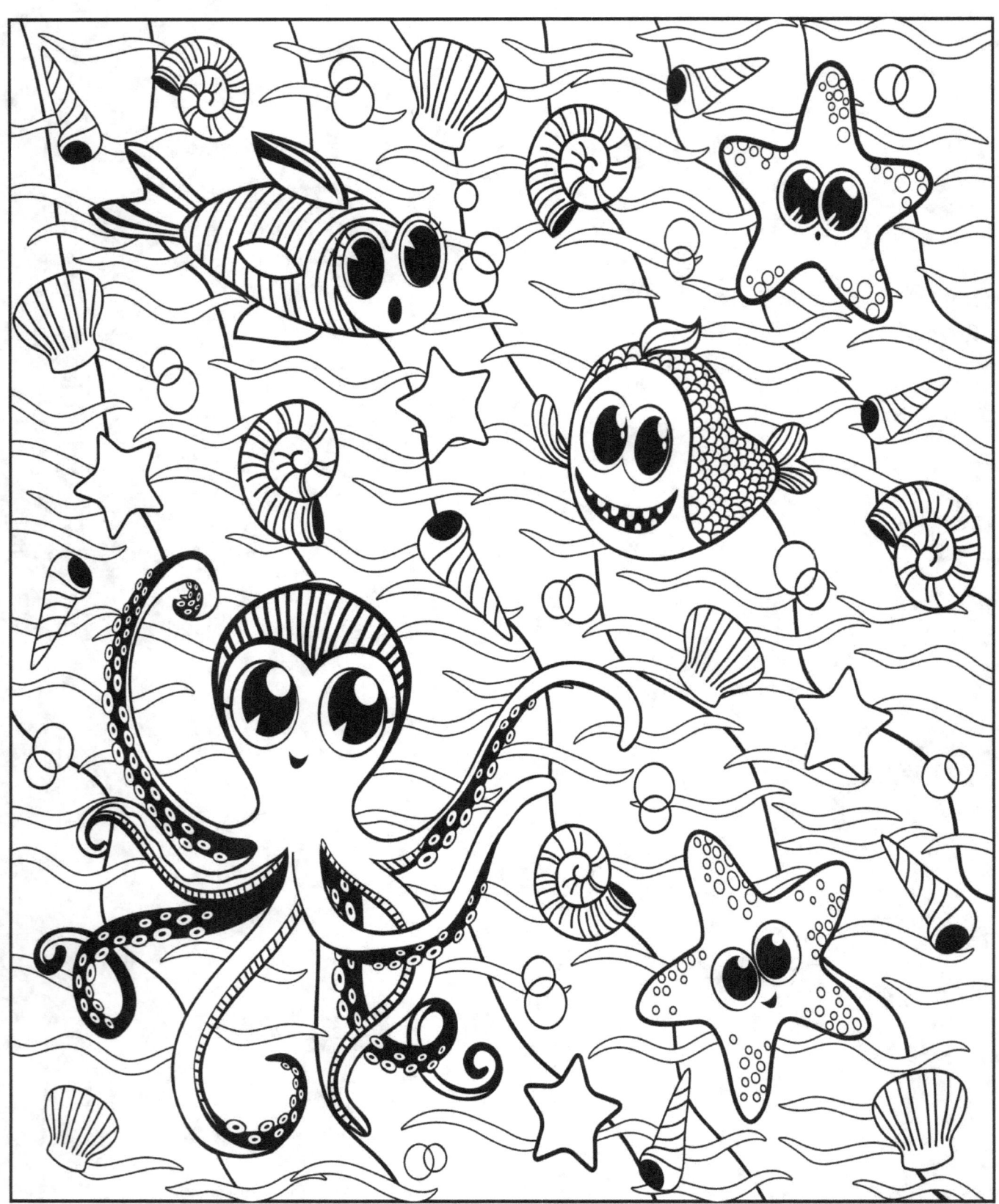

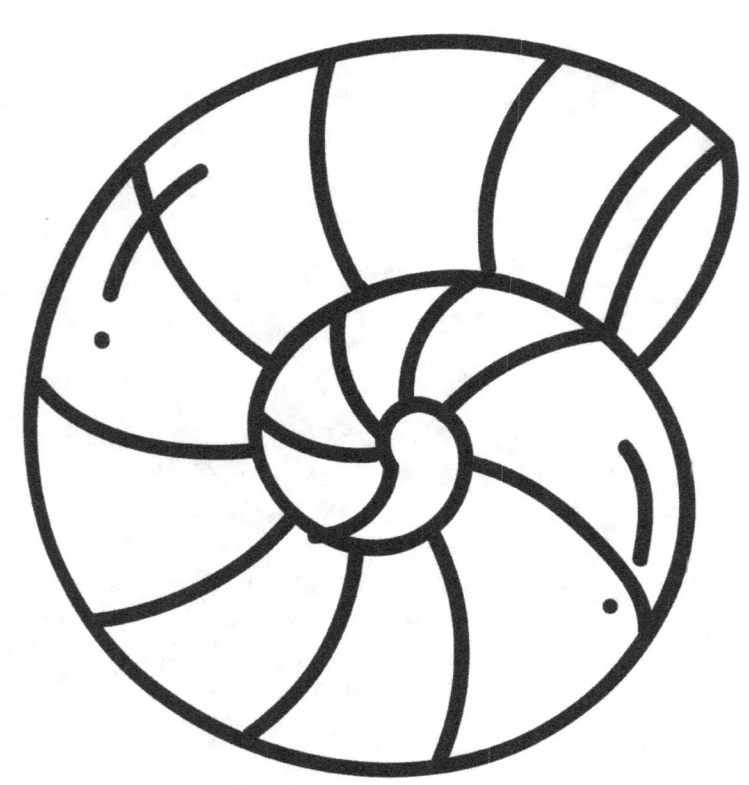

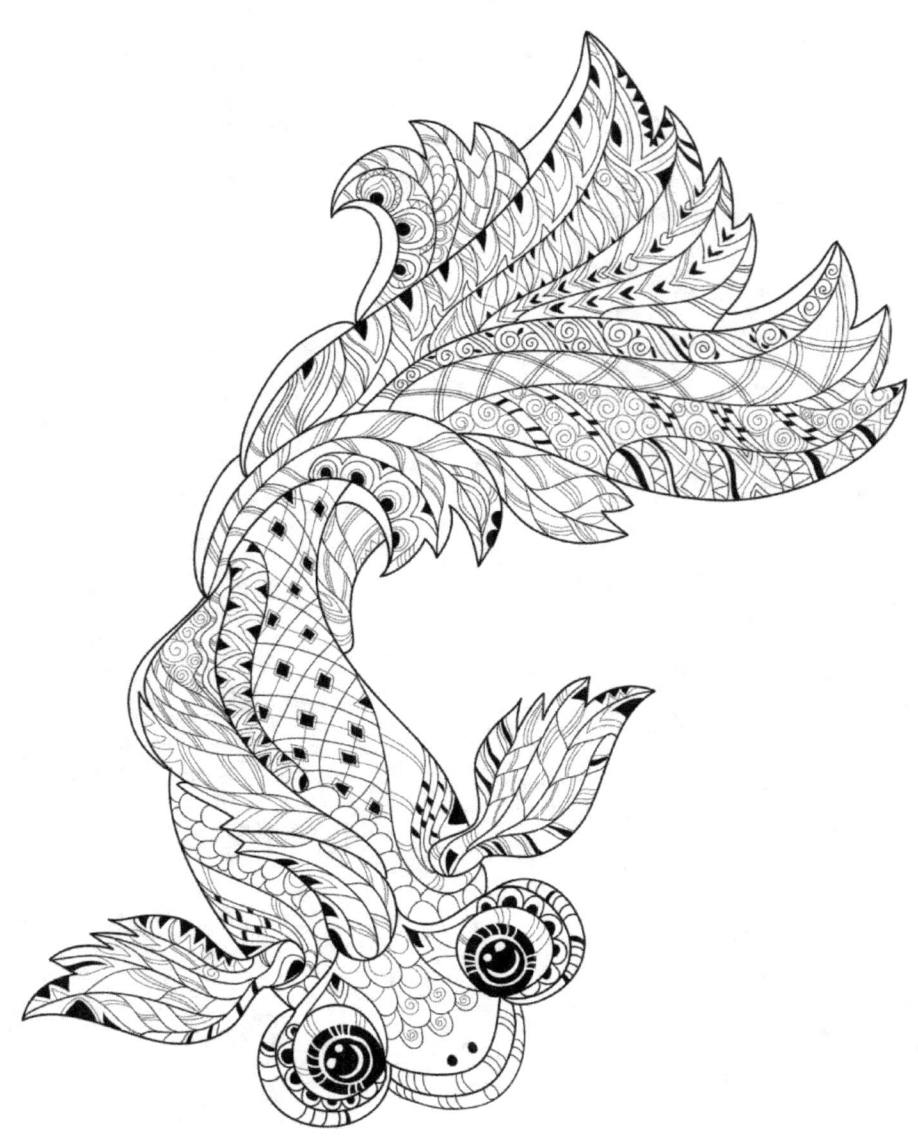

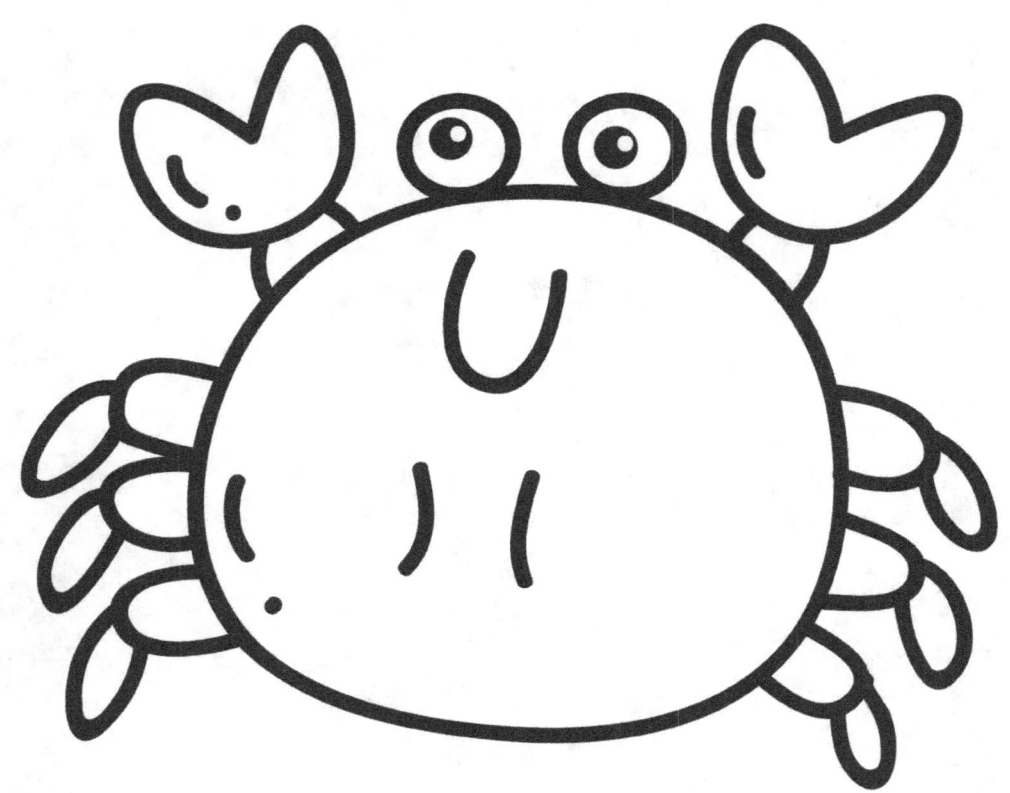

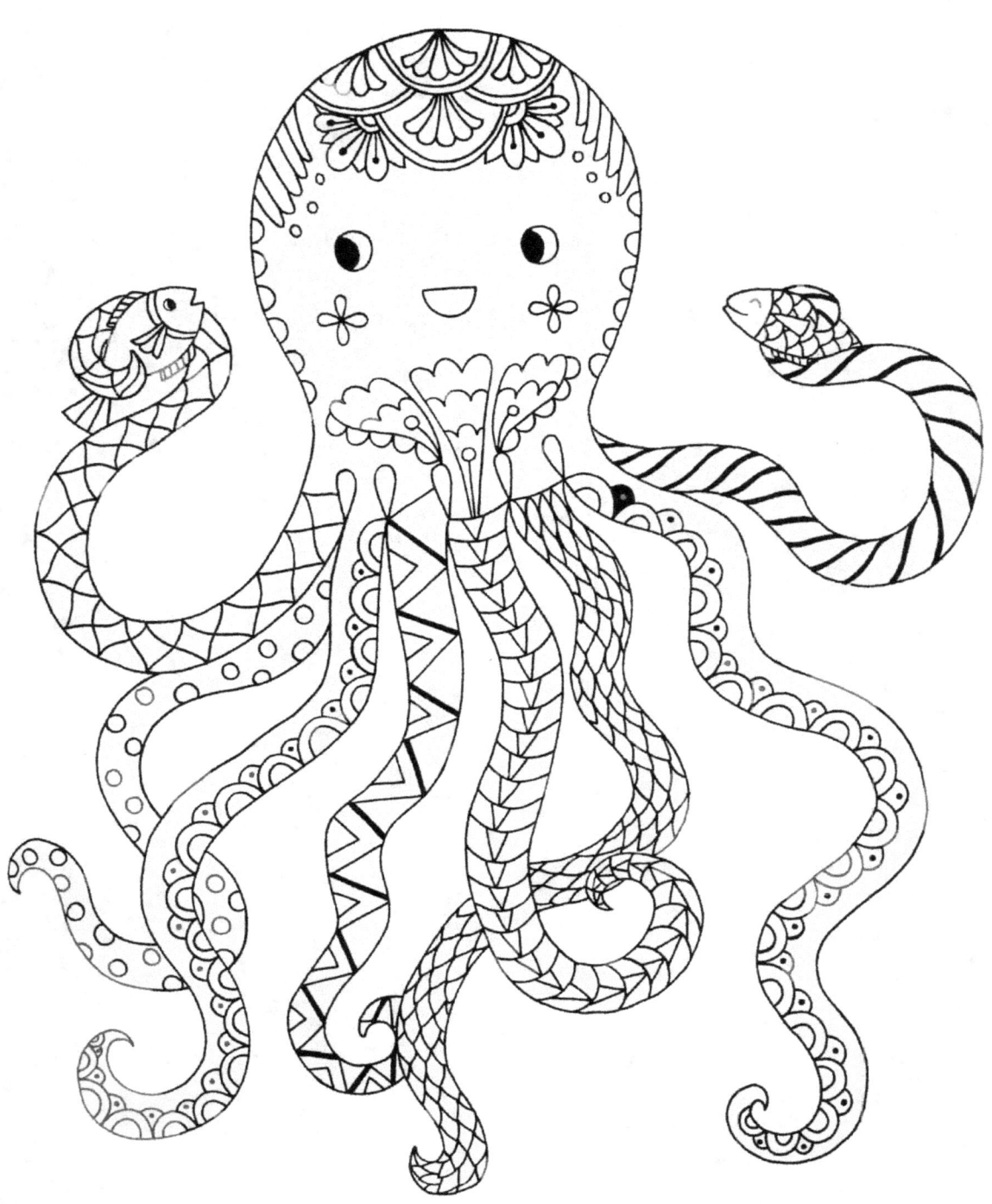

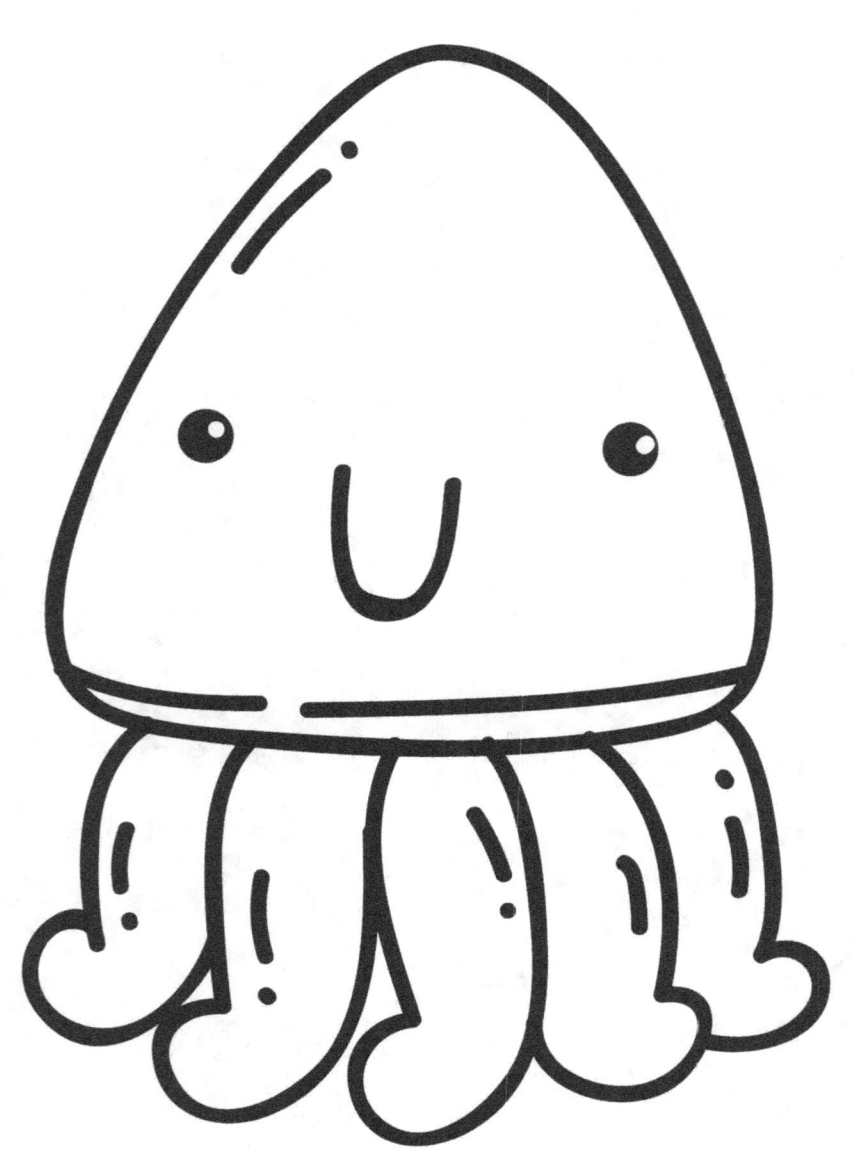

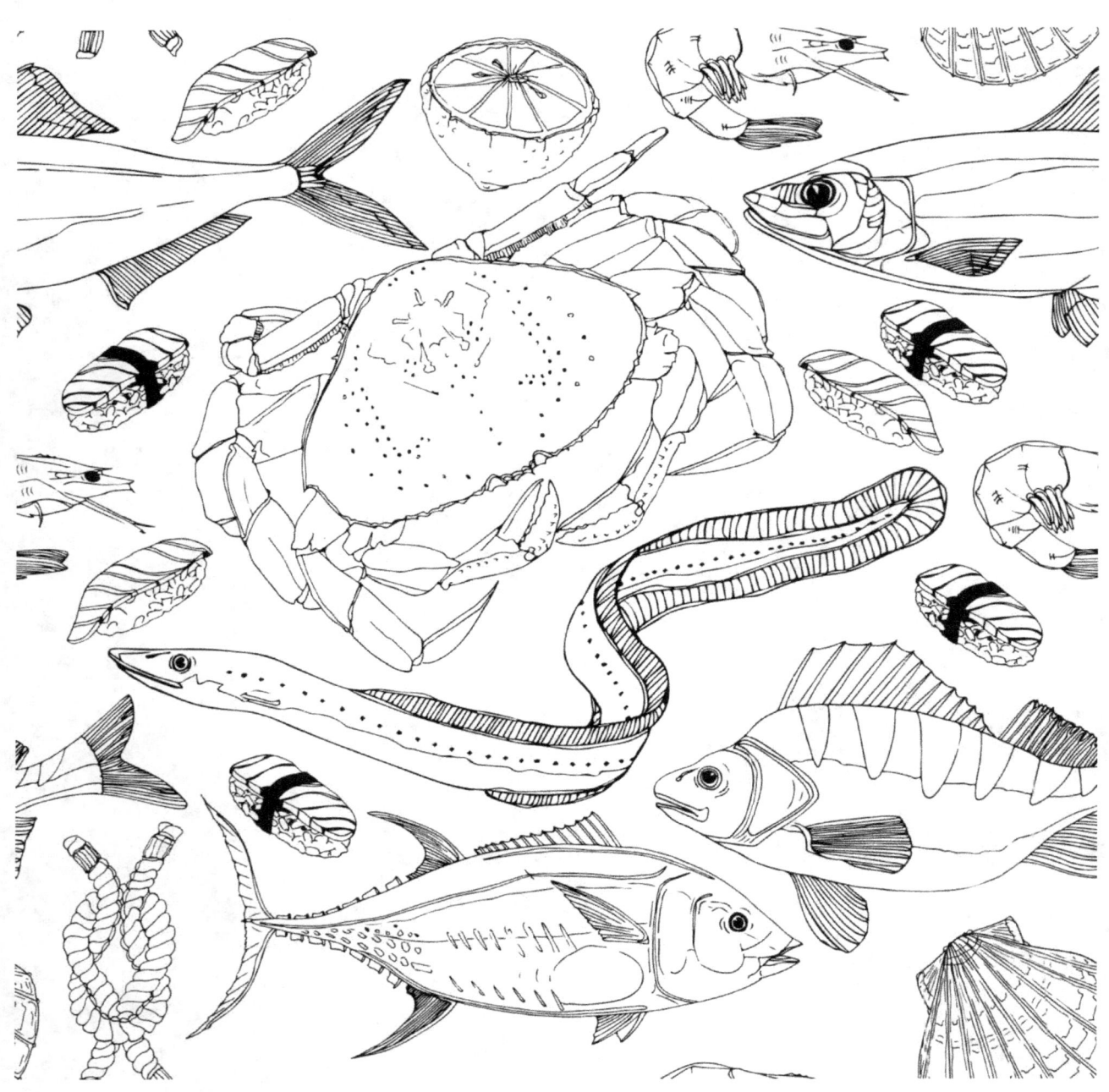

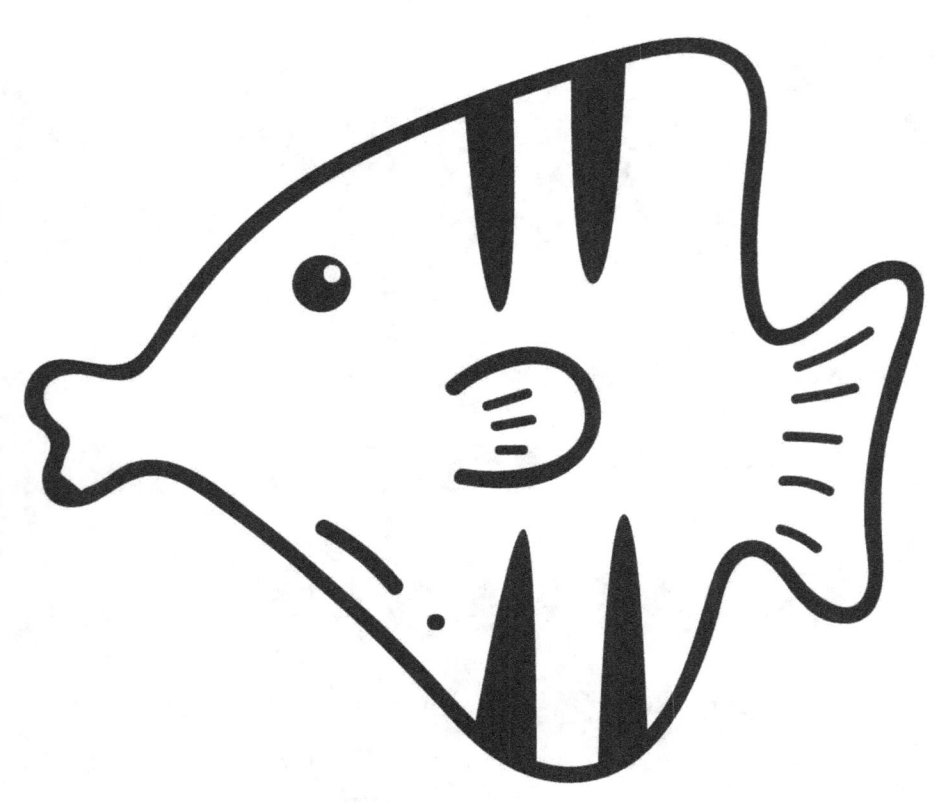

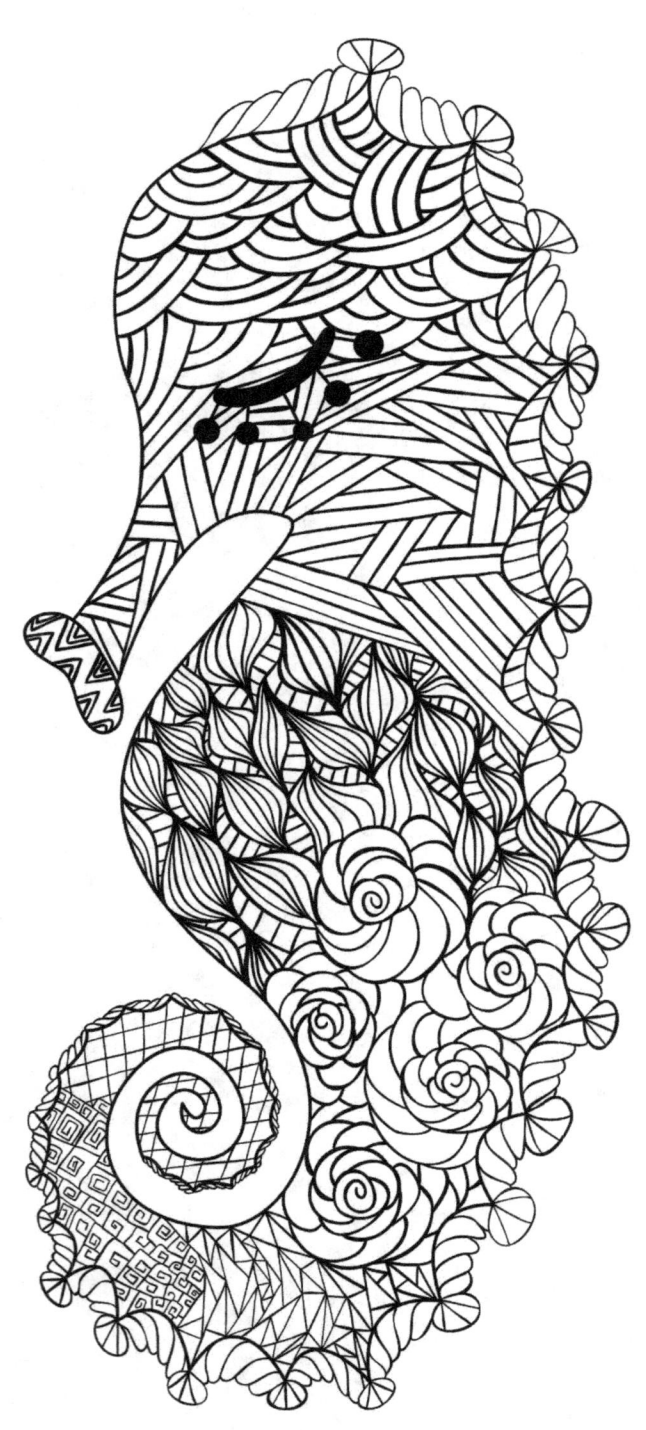

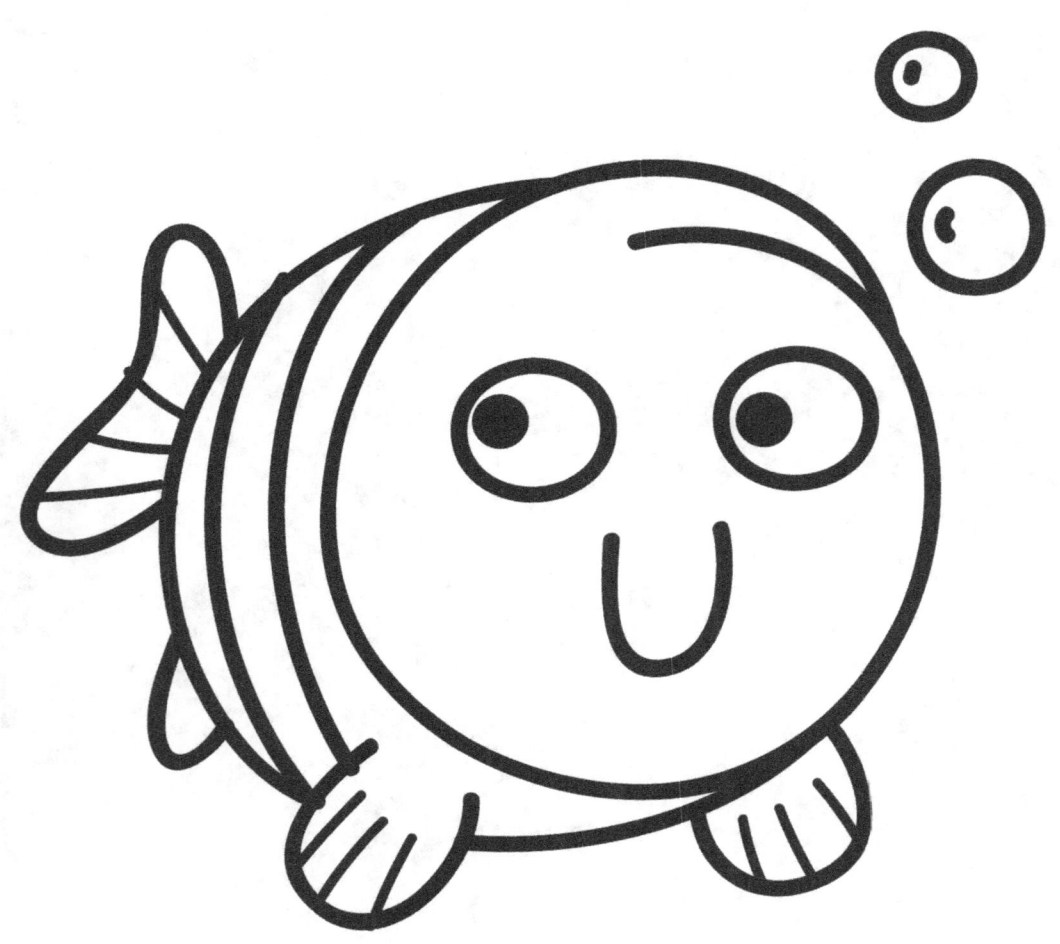

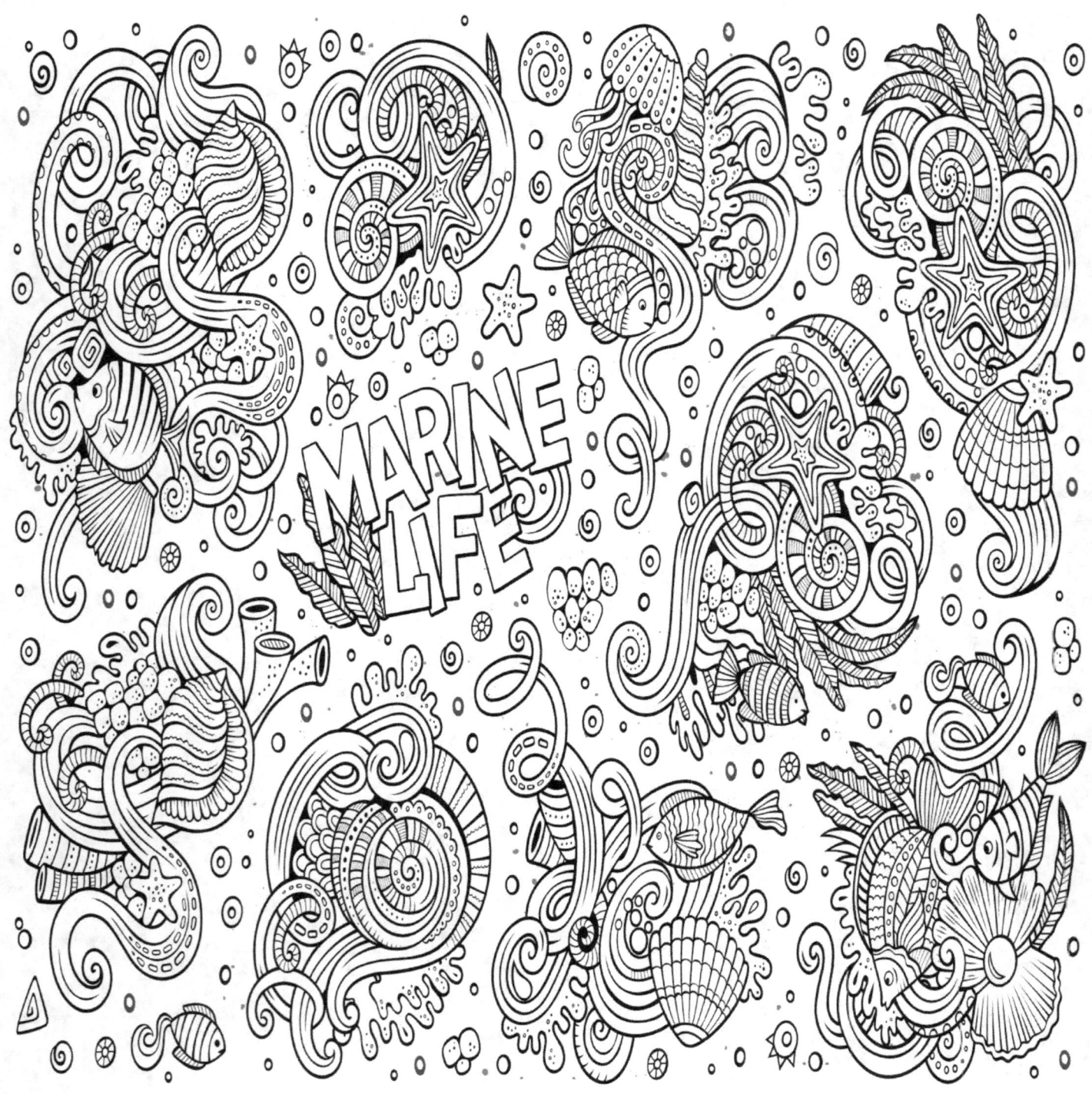

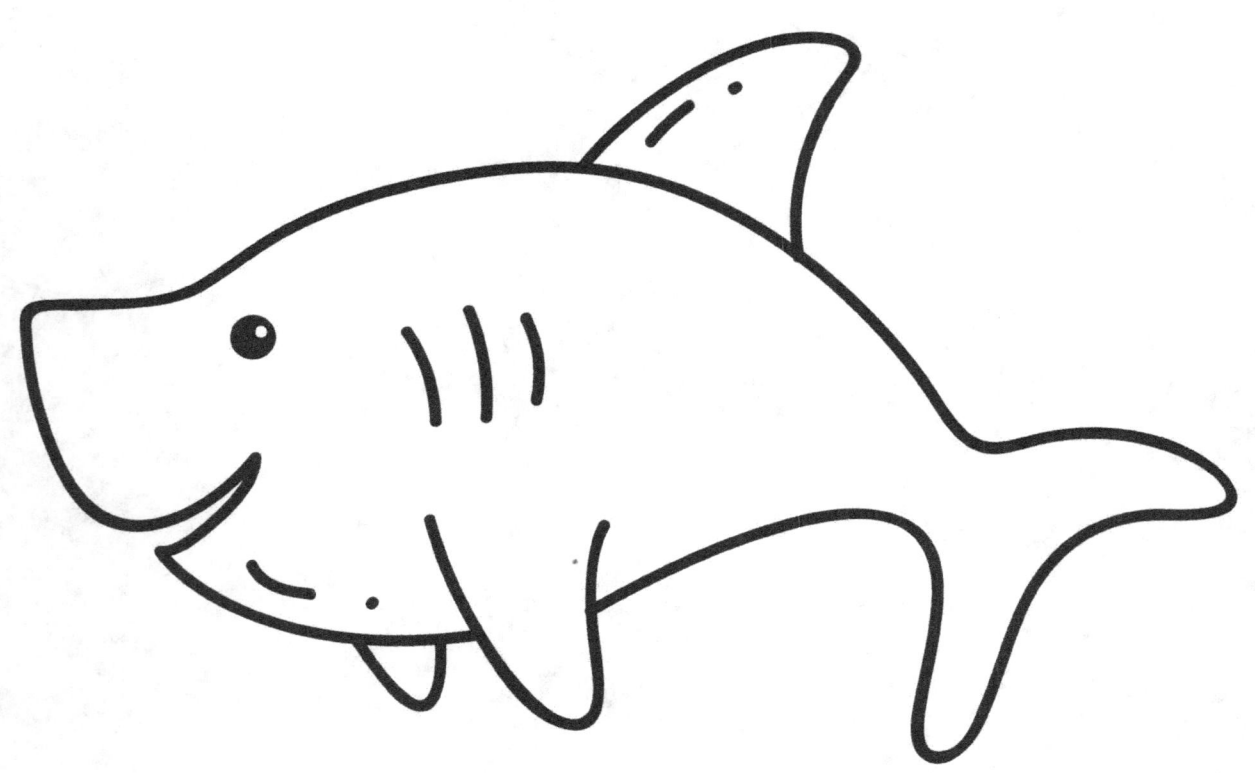

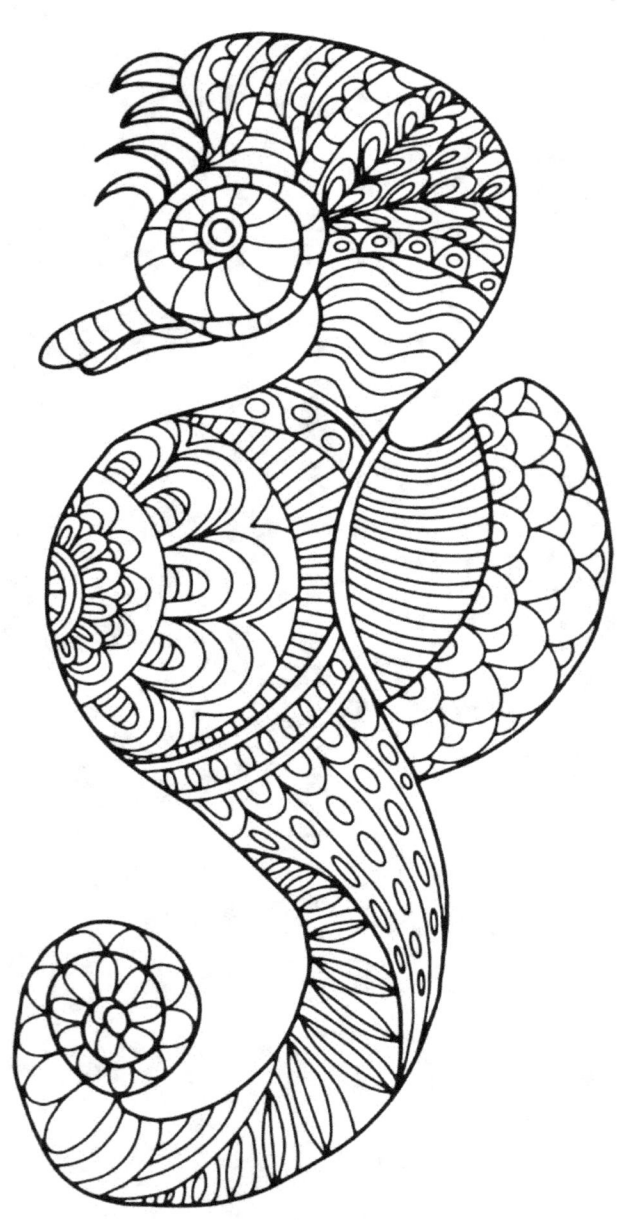

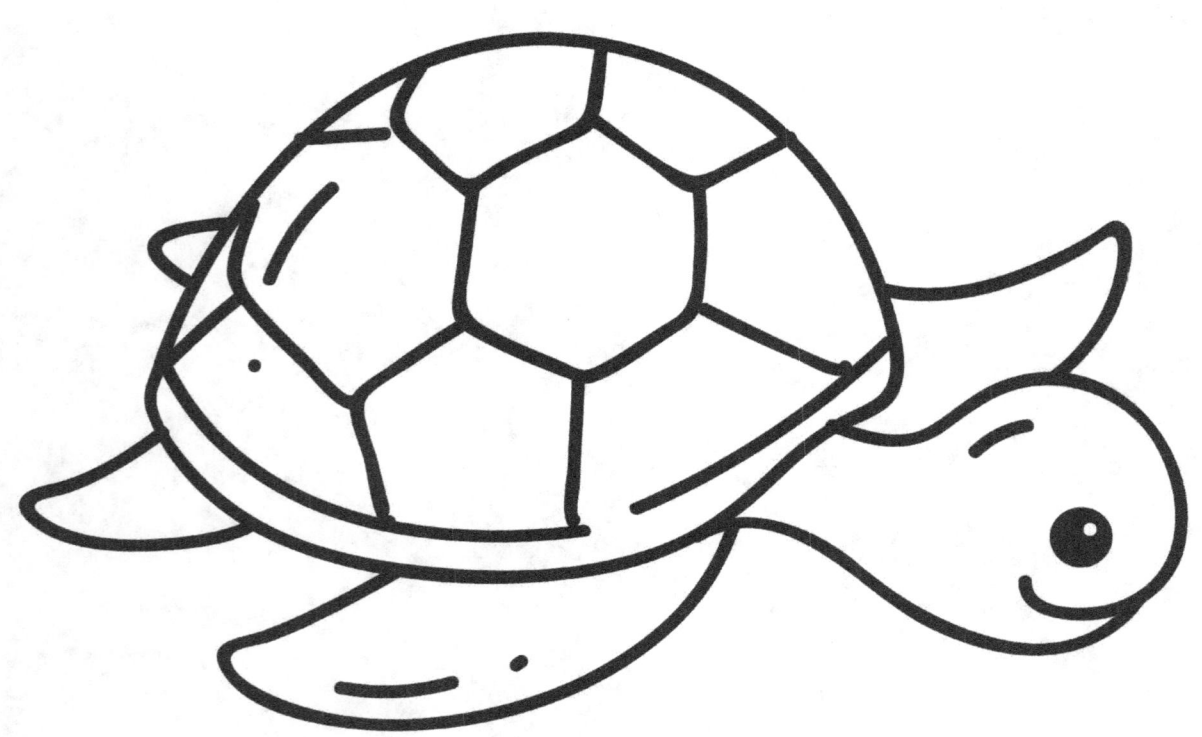

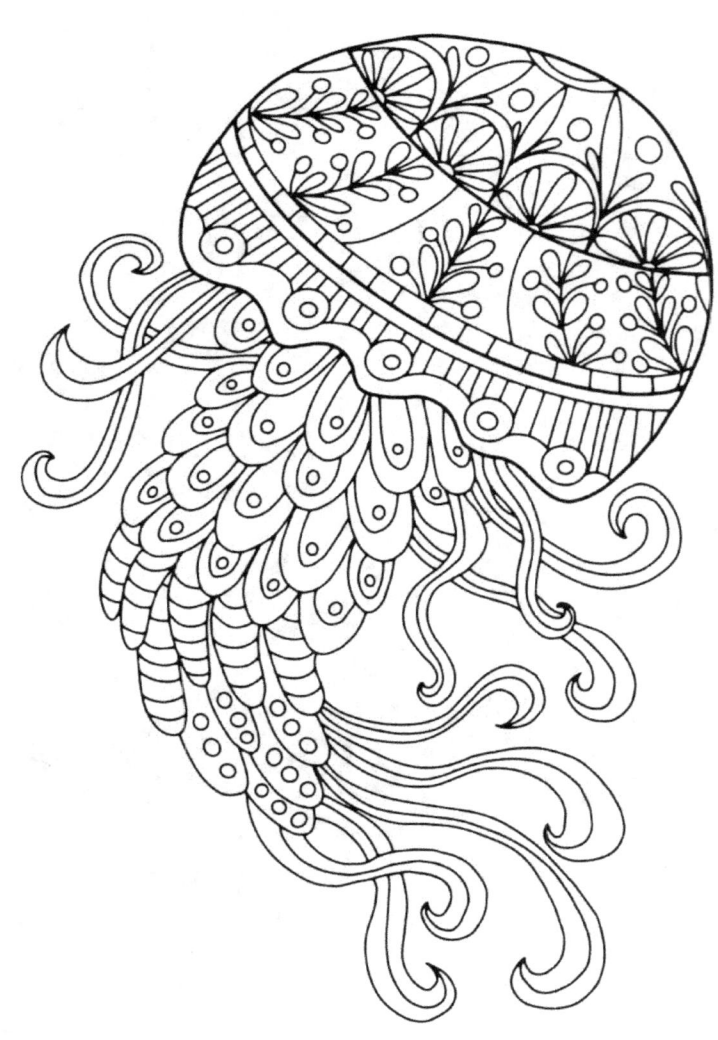

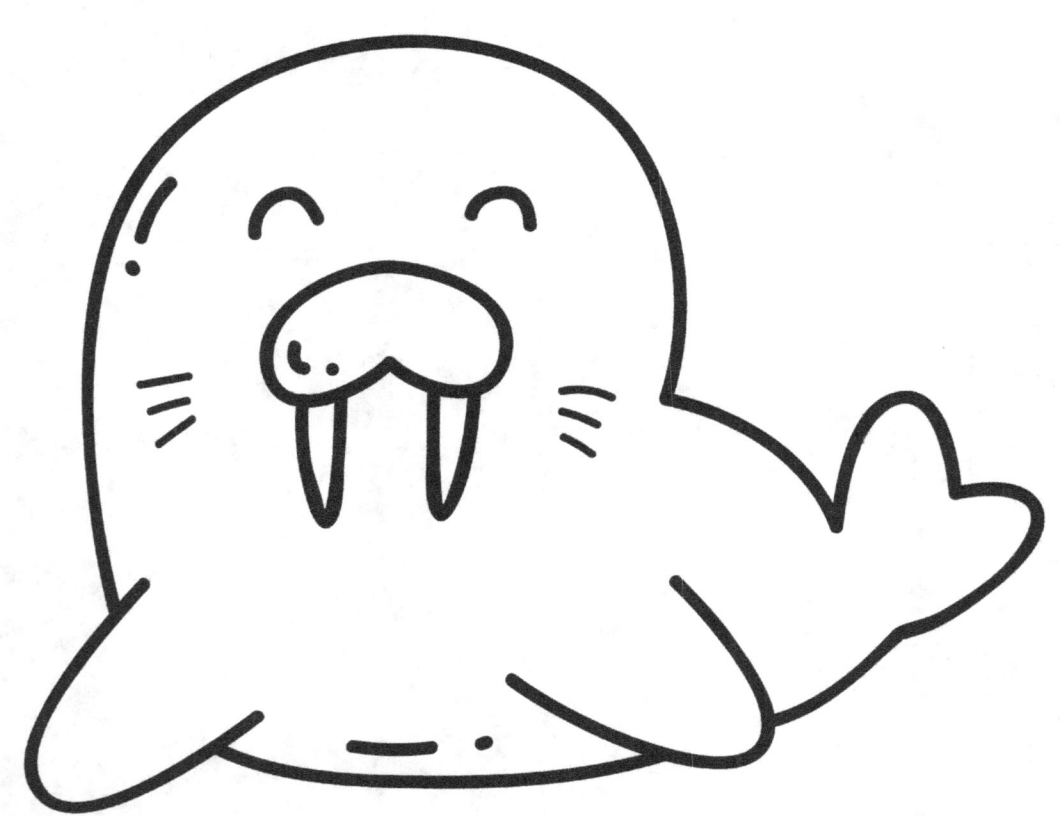

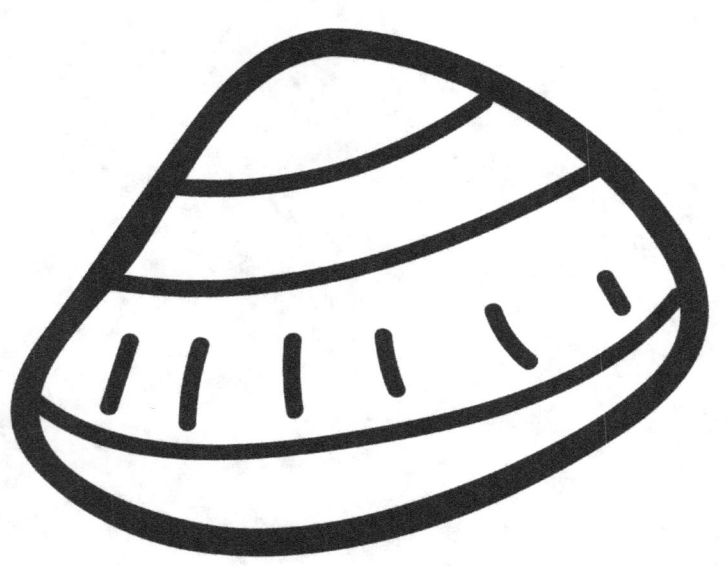

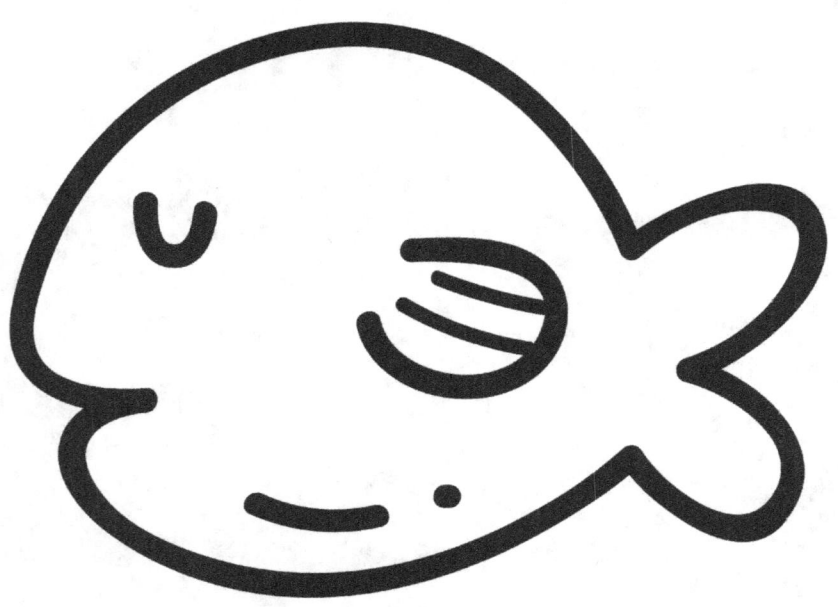

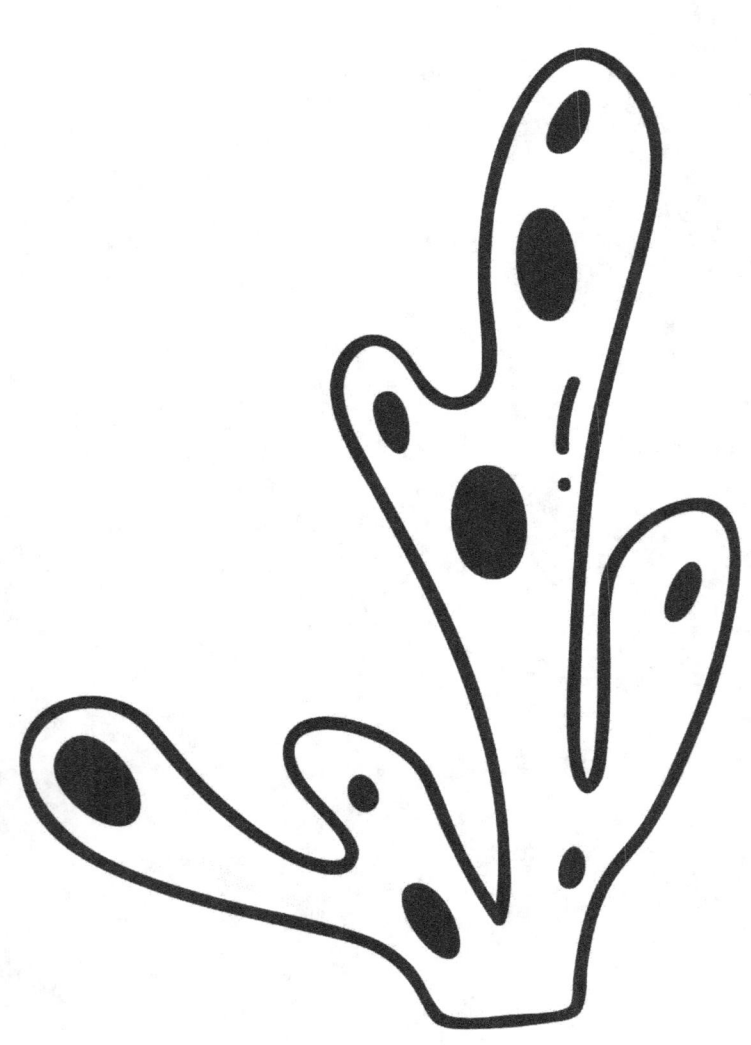

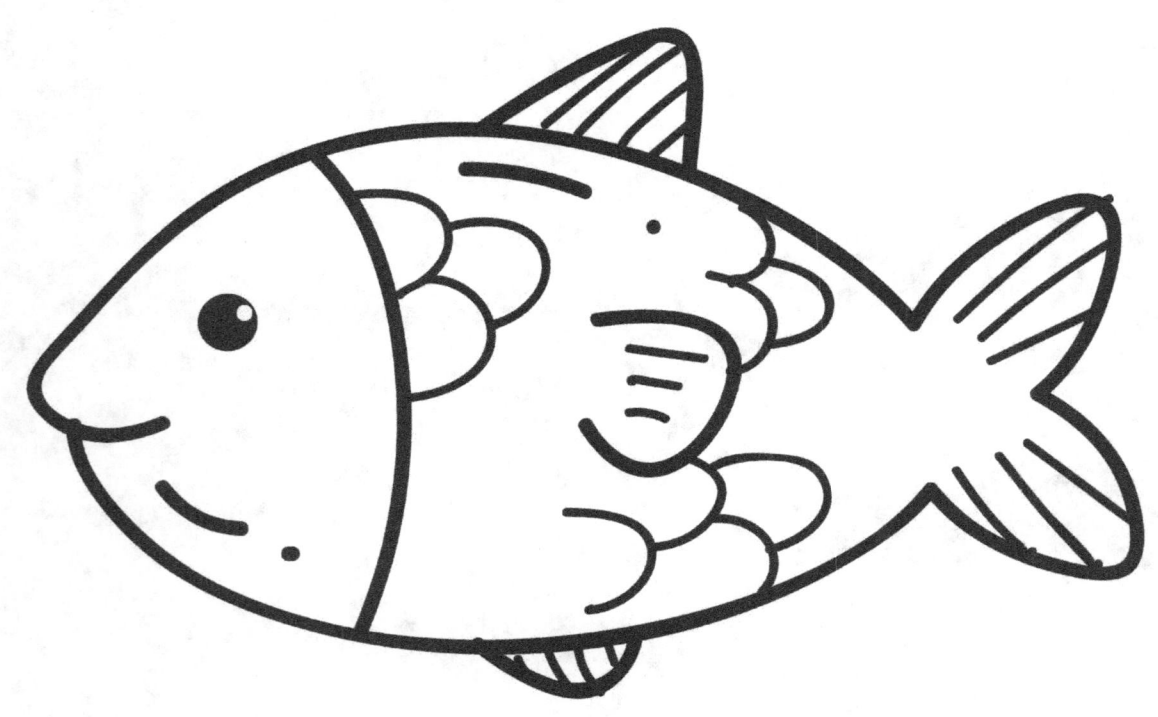

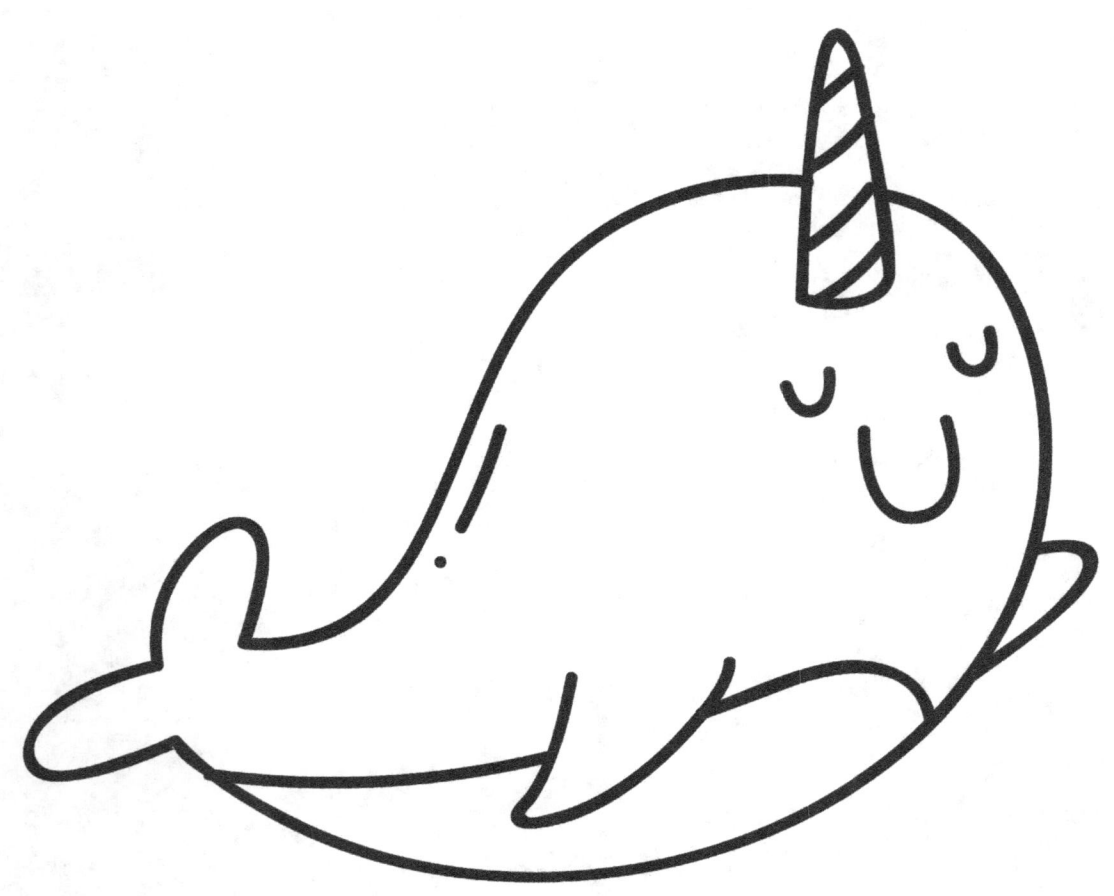

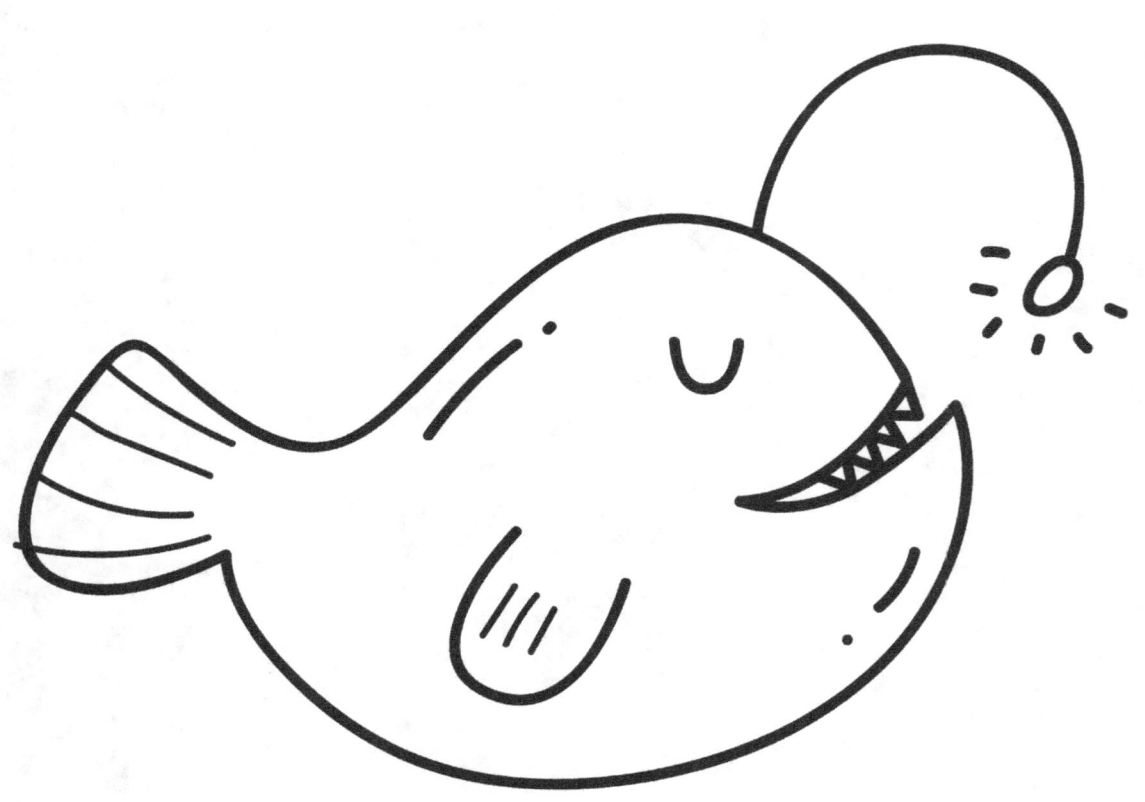

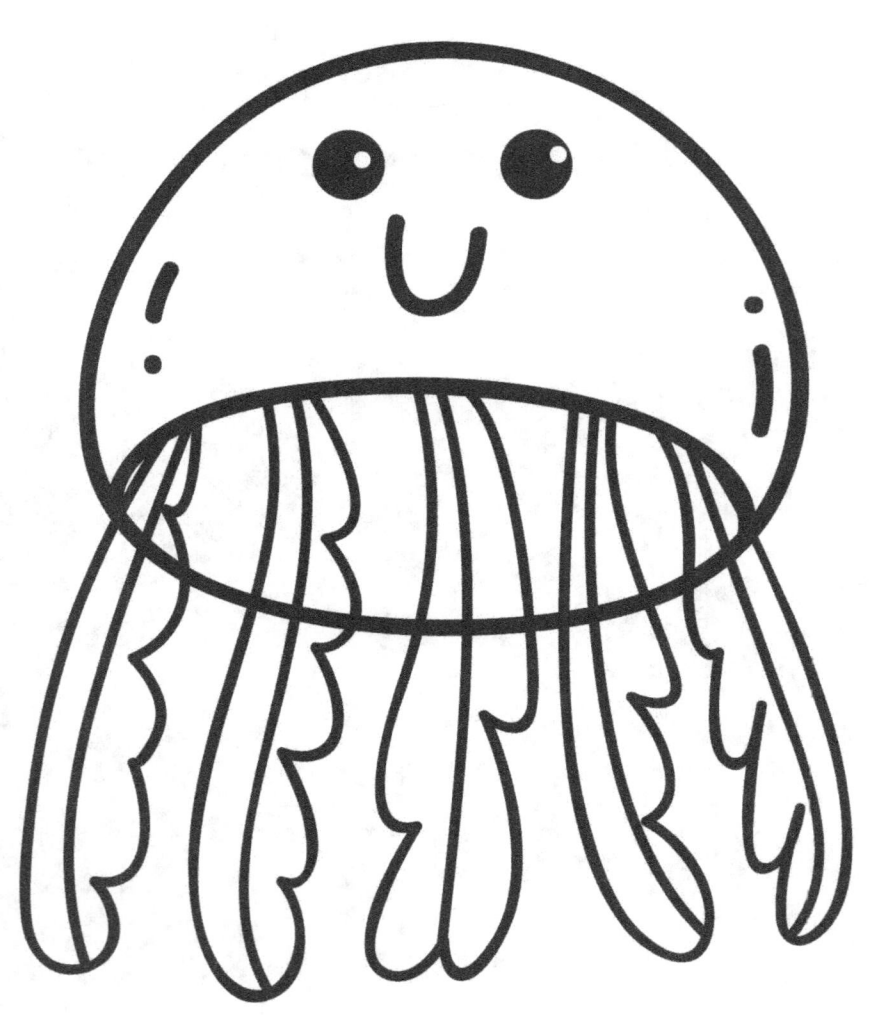

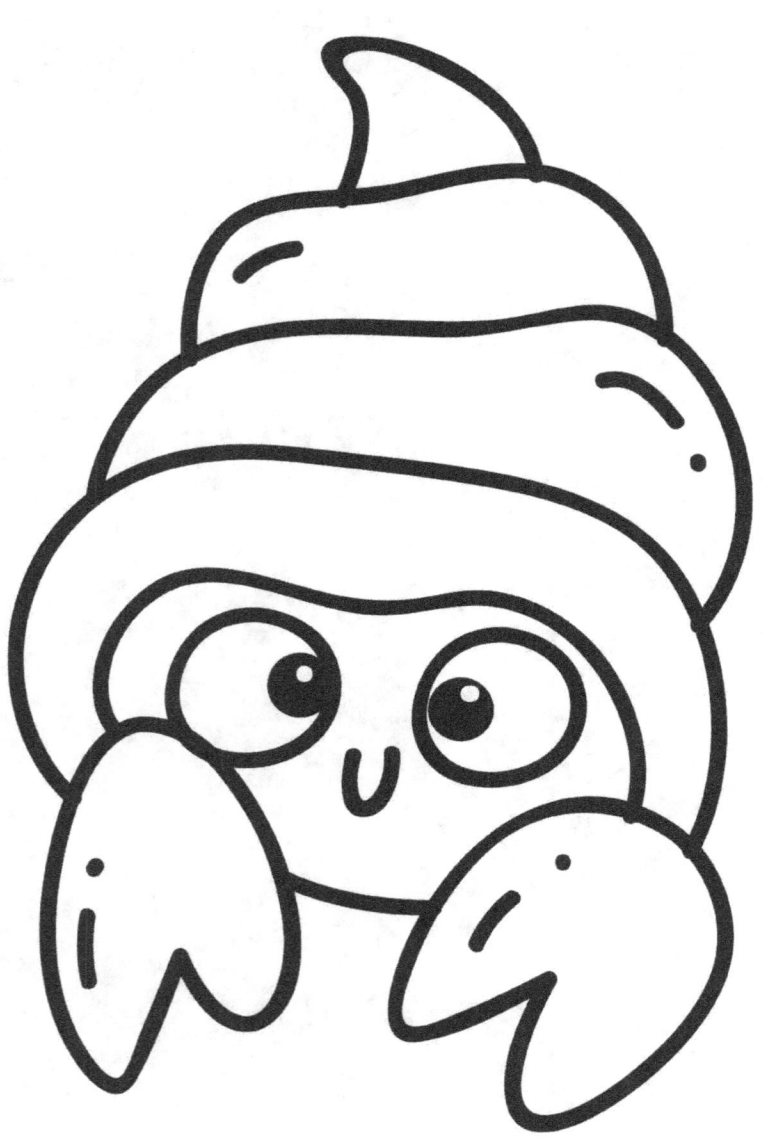

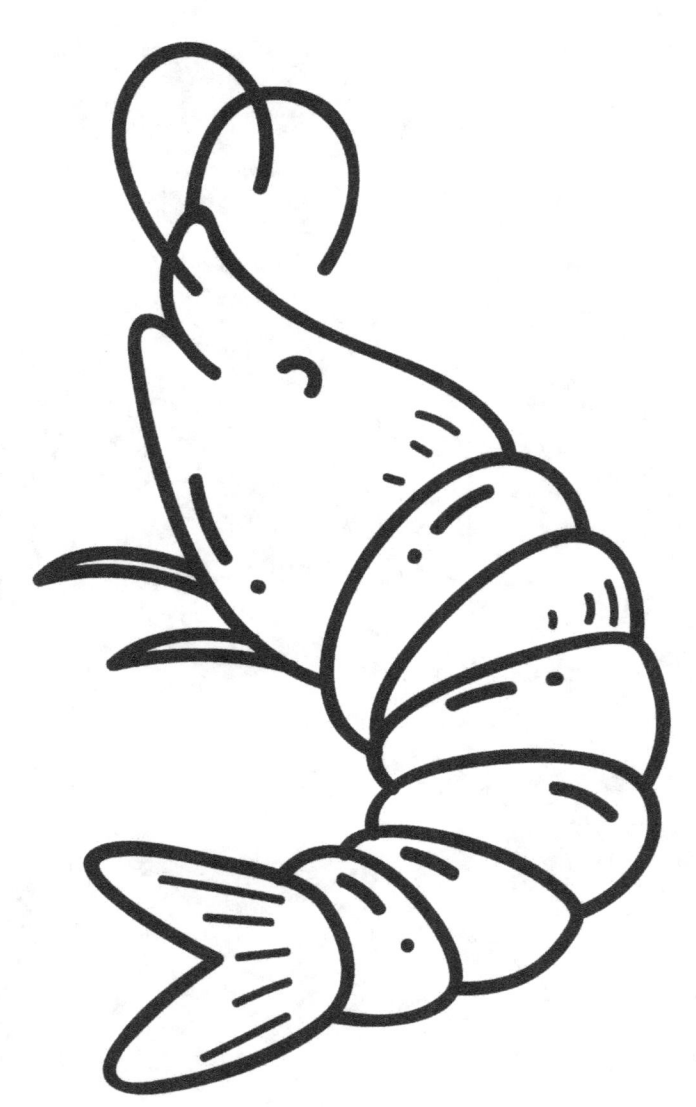

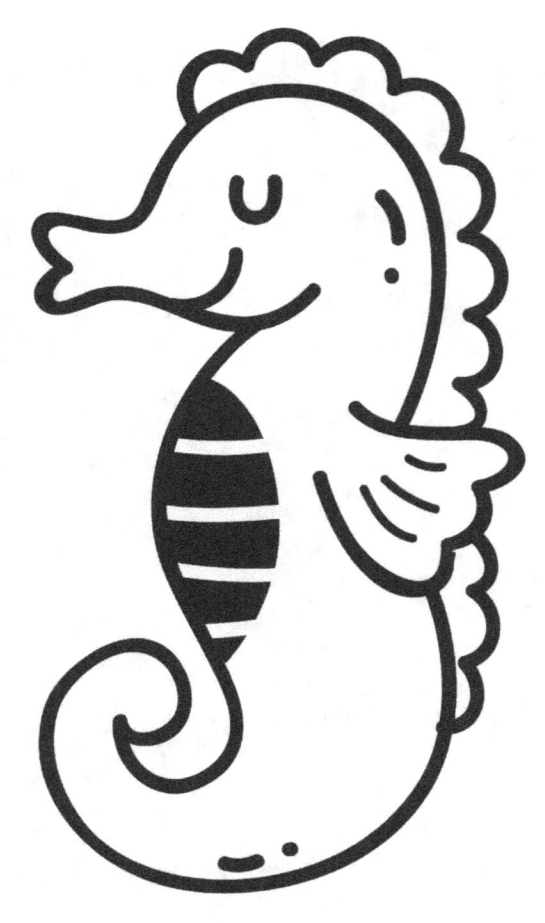

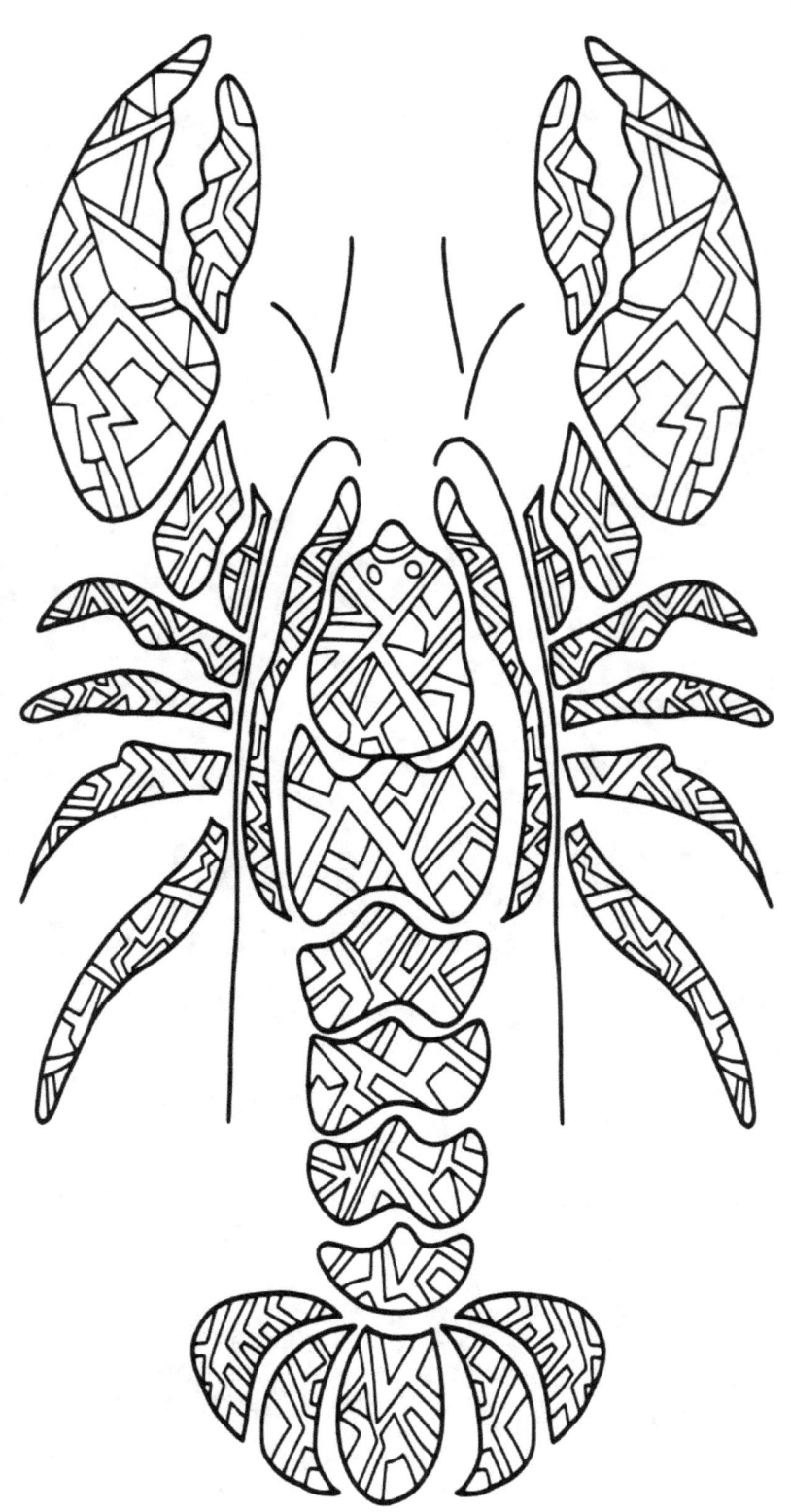

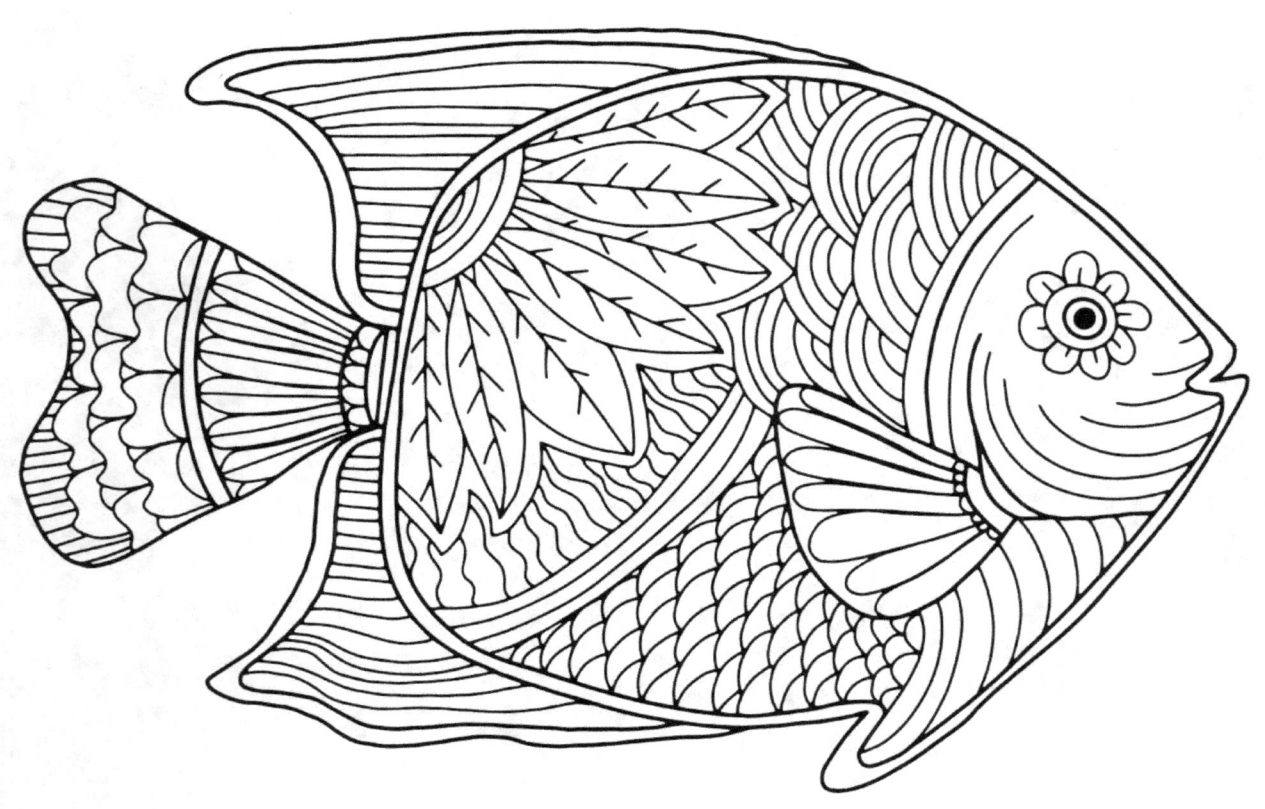

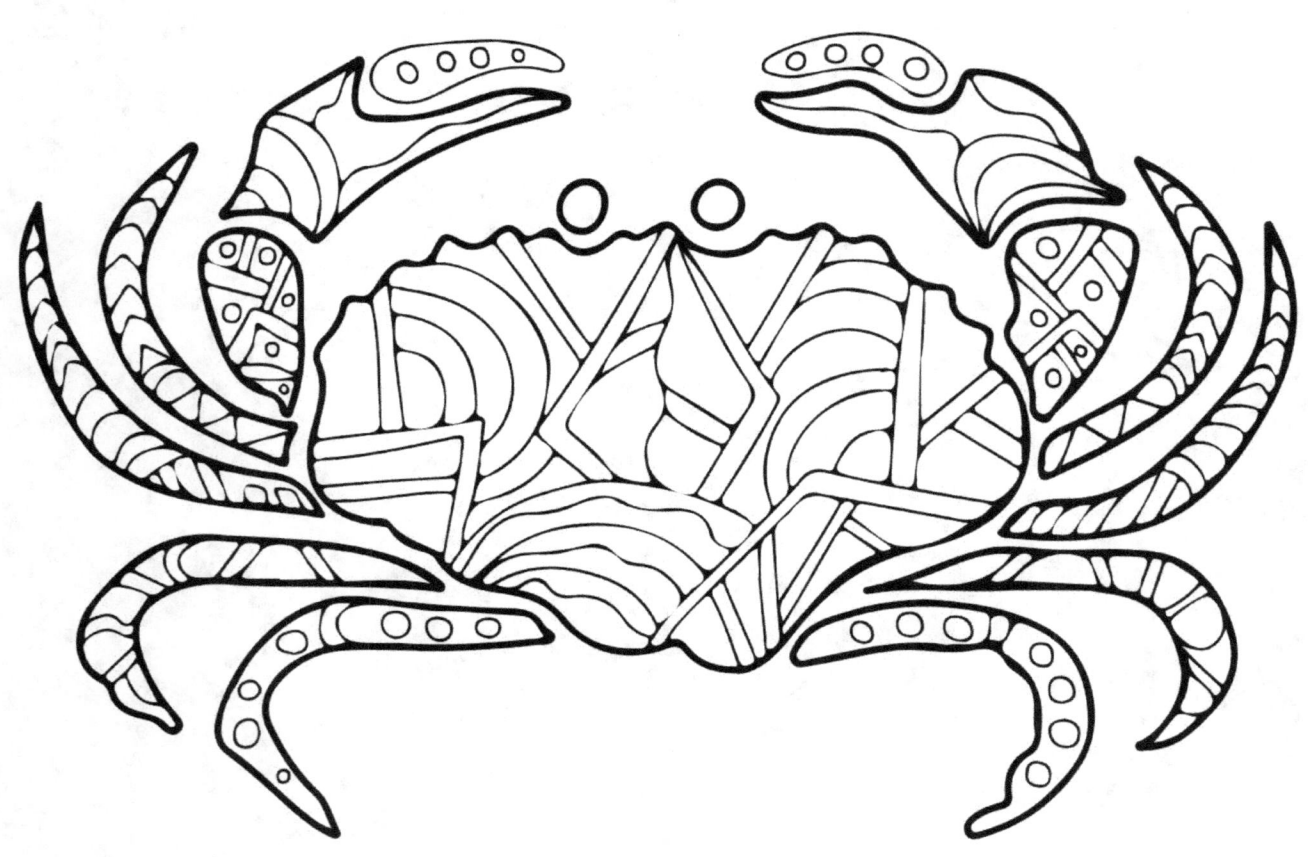

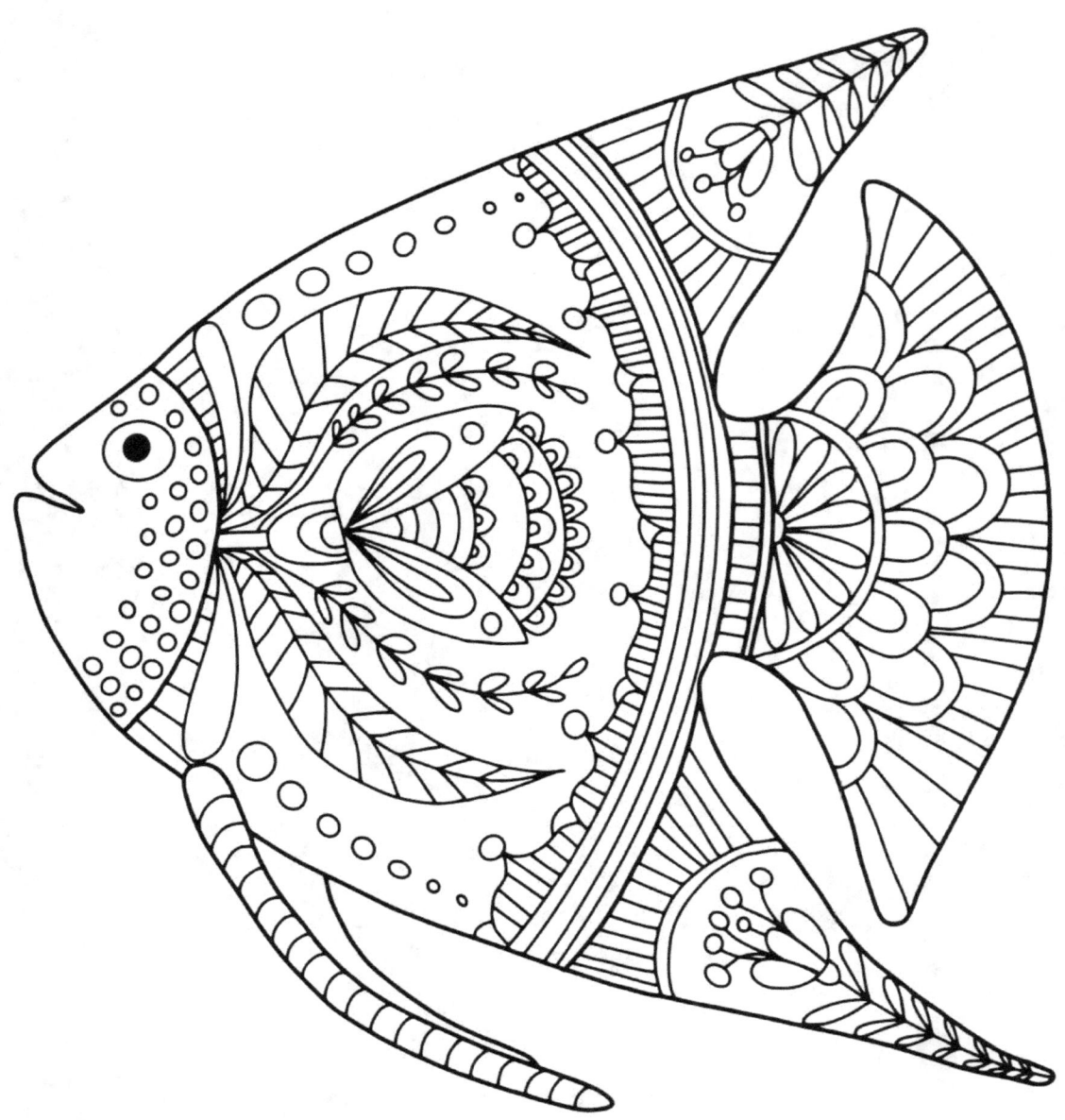

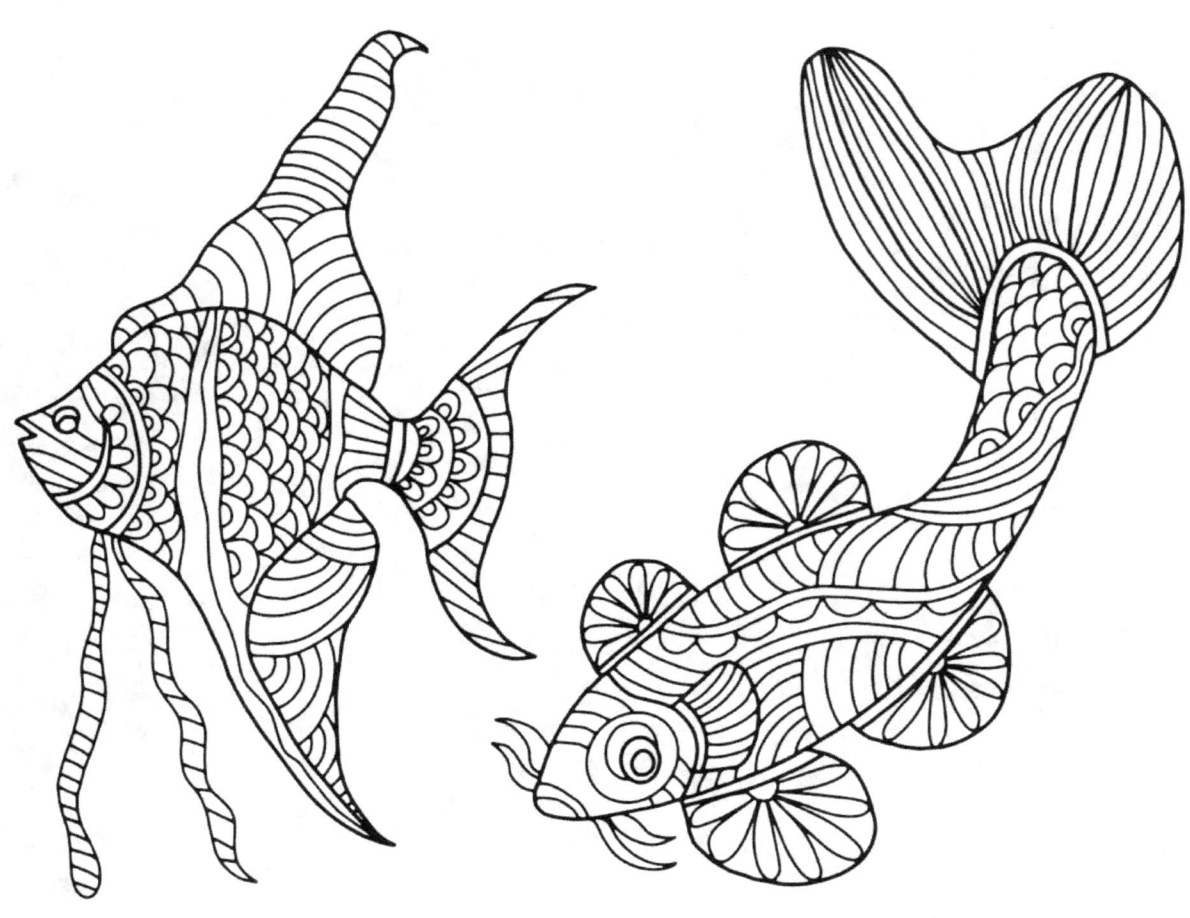

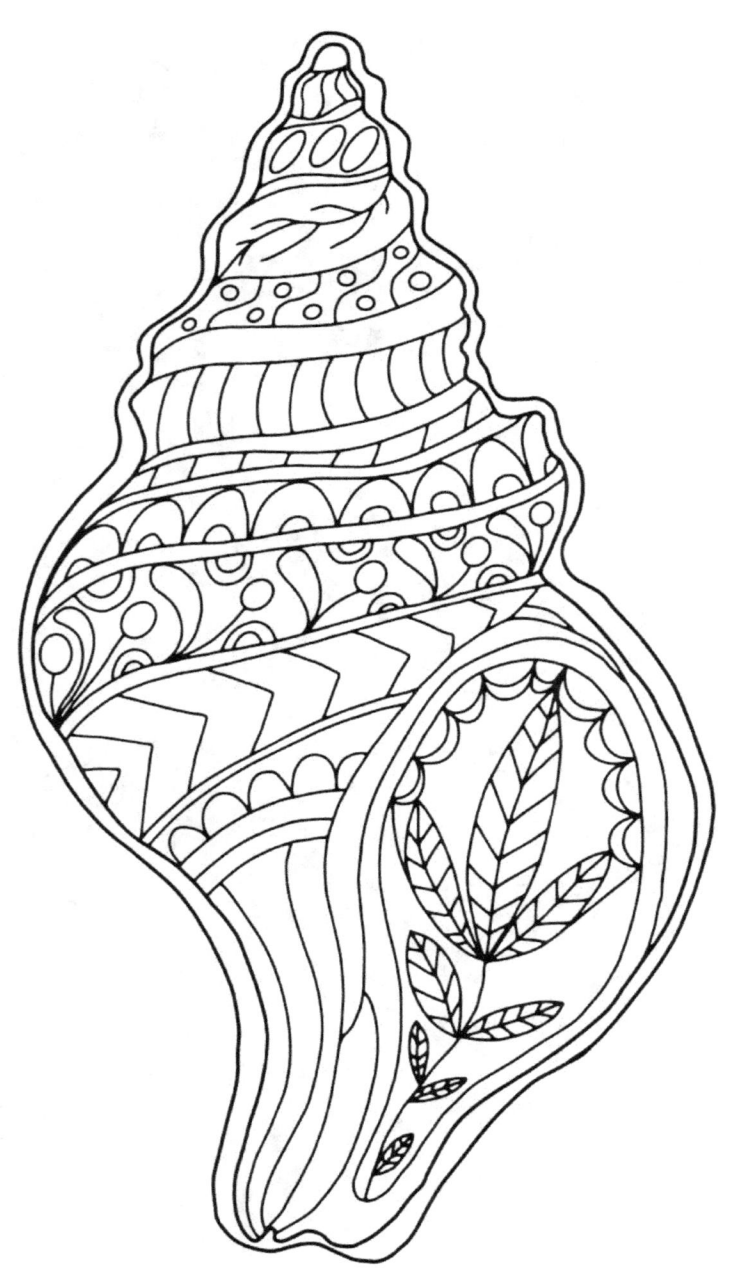

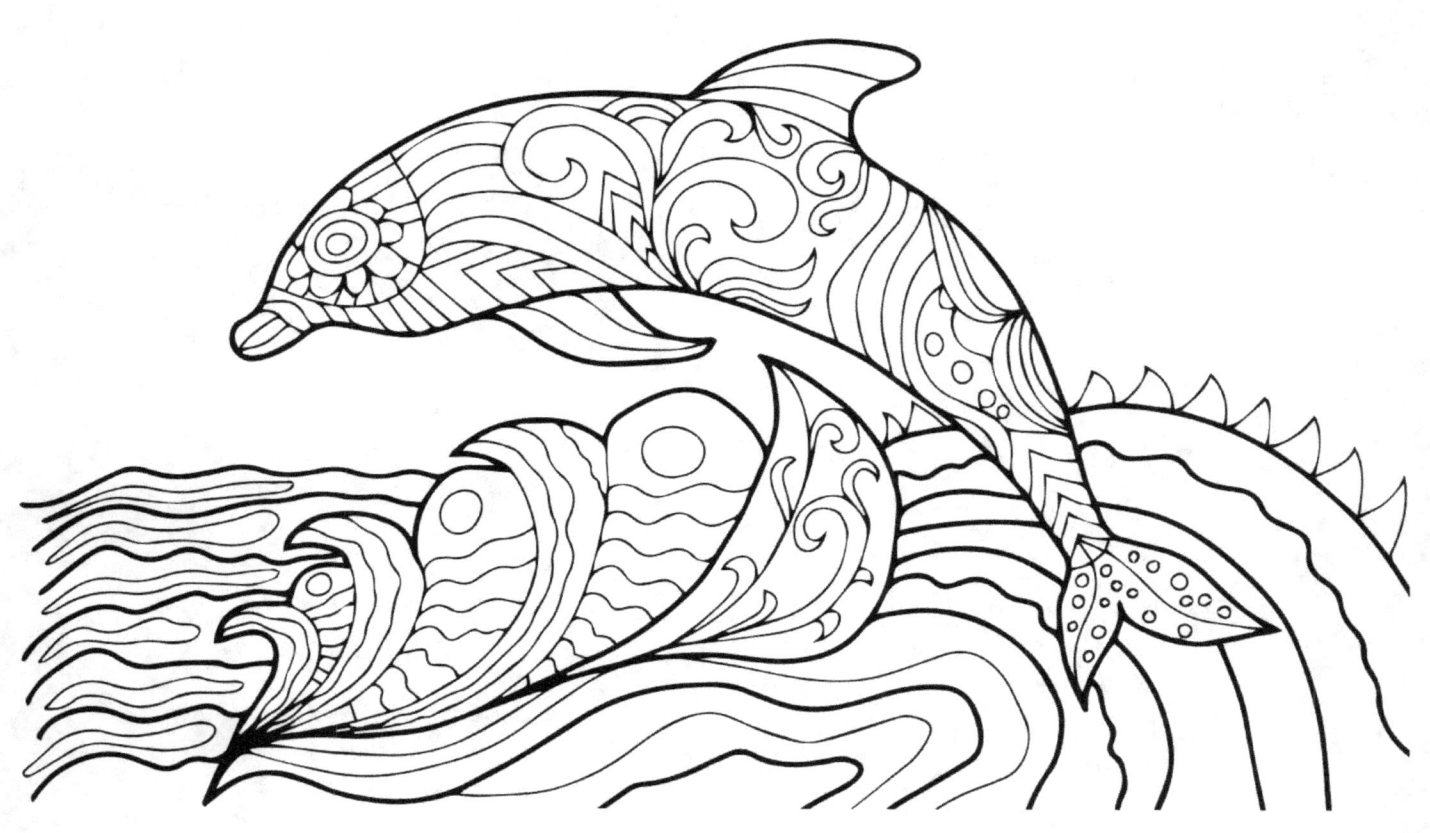

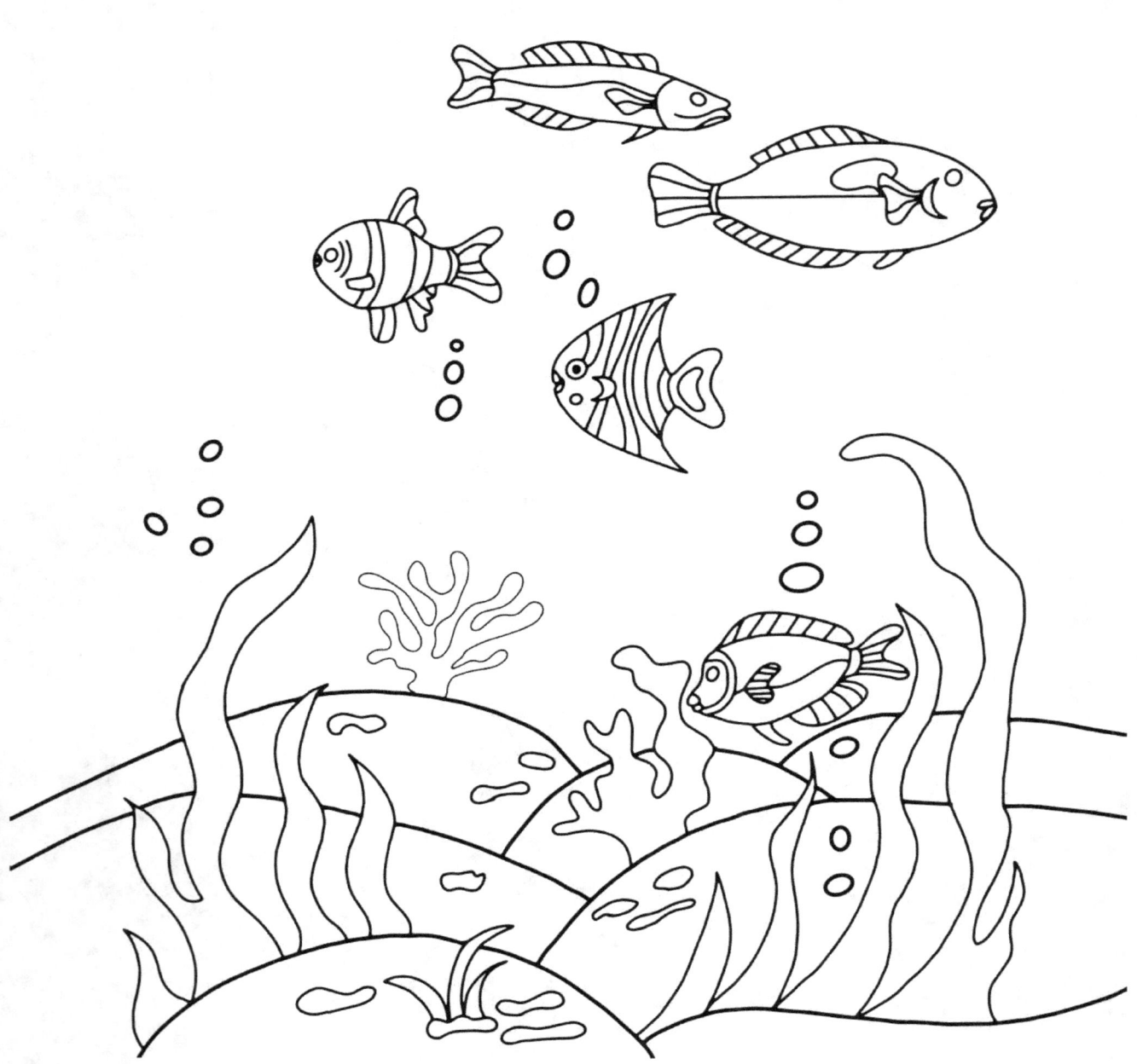

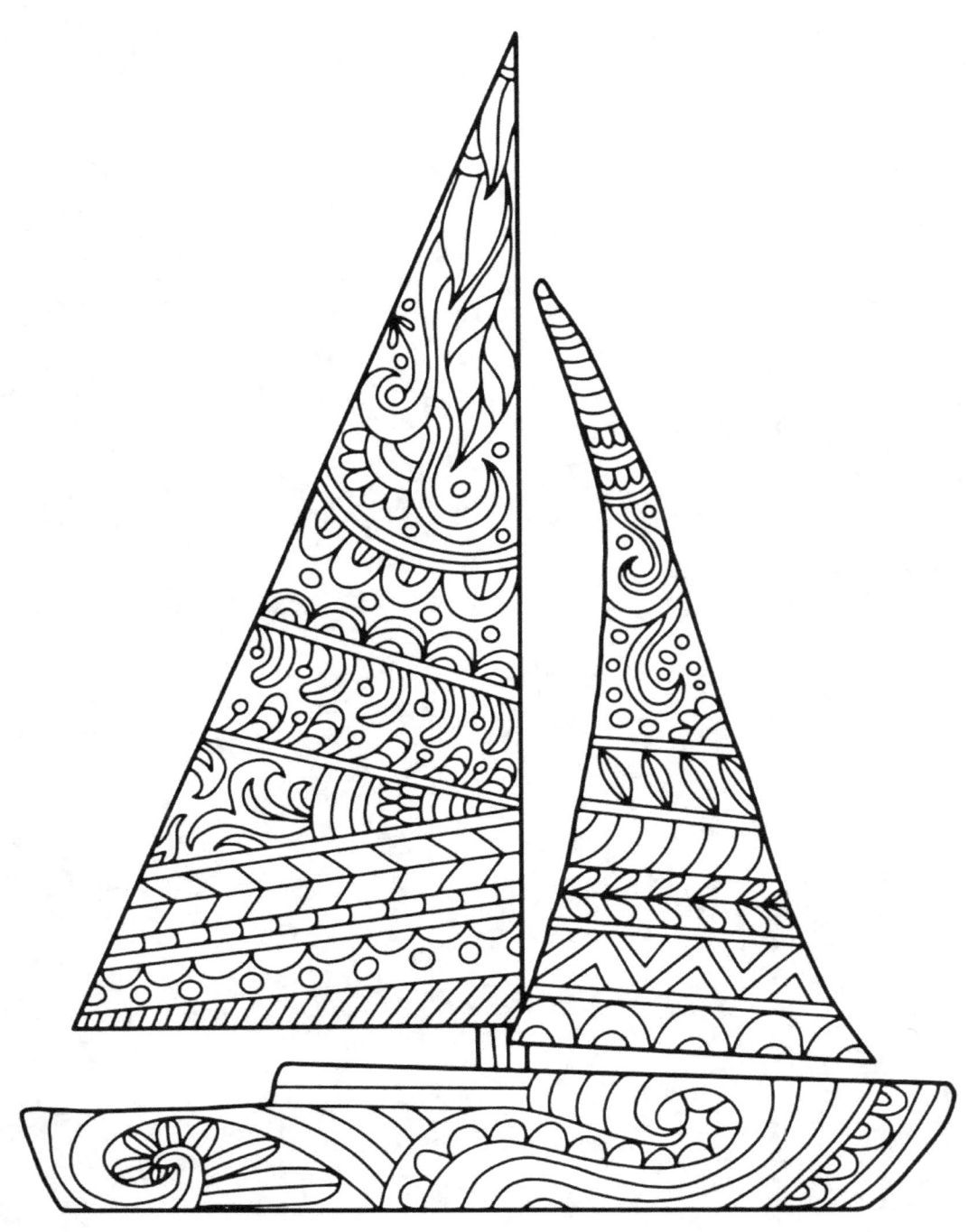

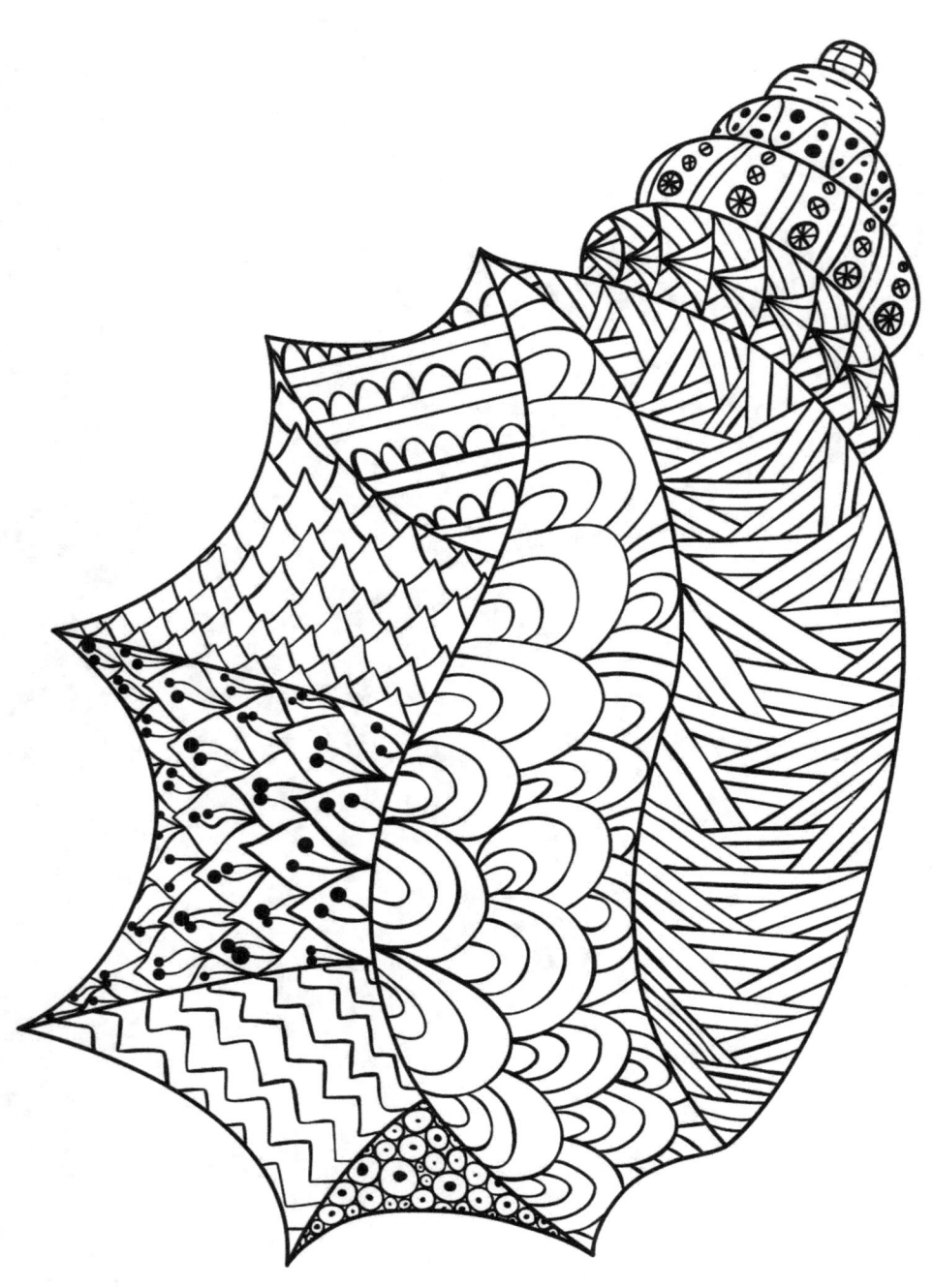

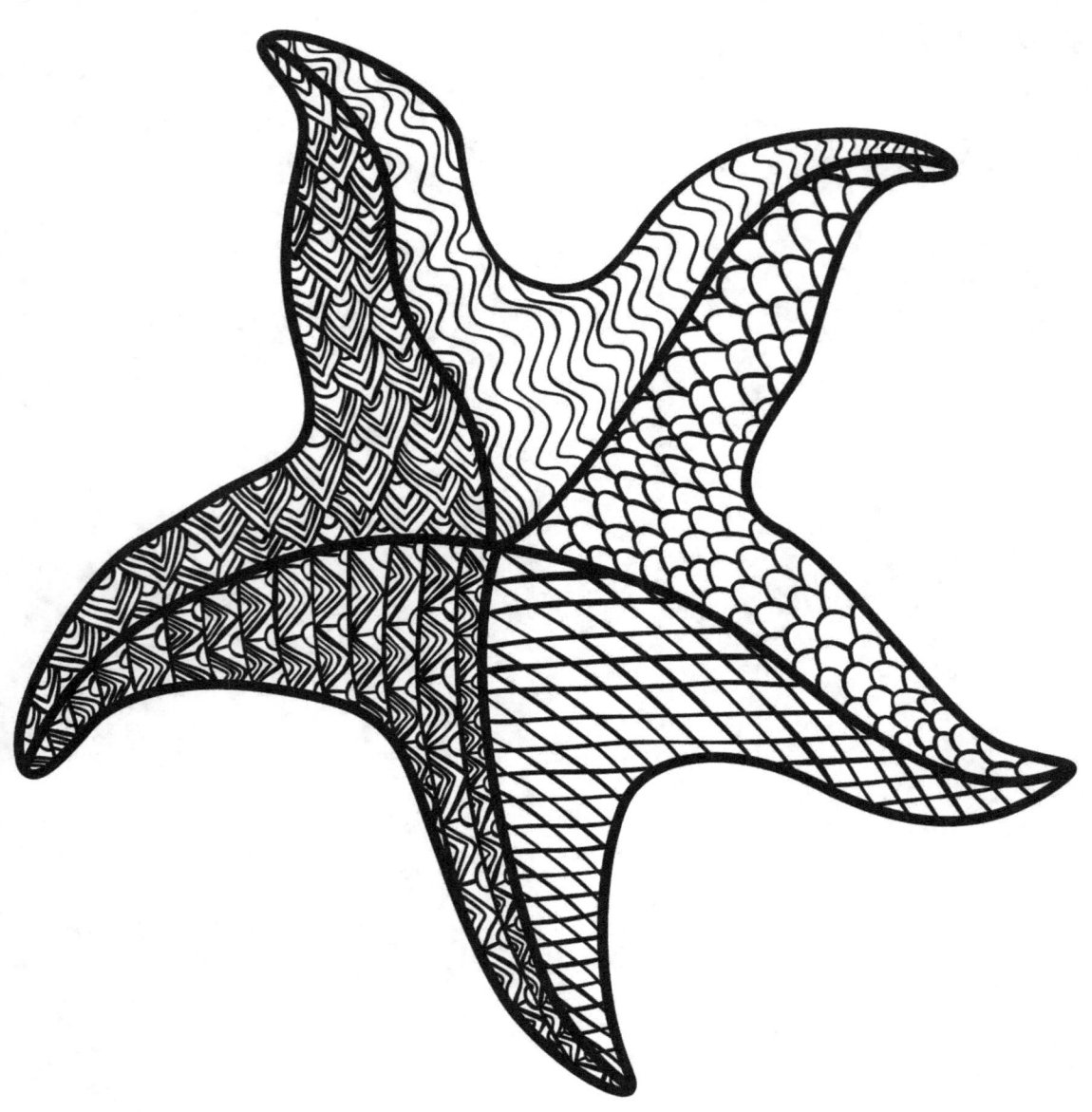